SURVIVAL GARDENING

Books on allied subjects by Edward Hyams

From the Wasteland
Soil and Civilization
Prophecy of Famine   (with Hugh Massingham)
Plants in the Service of Man
The English Garden
A History of Gardens and Gardening
Strawberry Growing Complete
Melons under Cloches
The Orchard and Fruit Garden   (with George Ordish)
The Grapevine in England
Vineyards in England
Dionysus: a History of the Wine Vine

SURVIVAL GARDENING

How to grow vegetables, herbs, fruit, nuts, wine and tobacco in garden or allotment

EDWARD HYAMS

JOHN MURRAY

Printed in Great Britain by Martin's of Berwick

CASED 0 7195 3404 6
PAPERBACK 0 7195 3409 7

CONTENTS

PART 1   BASIC TECHNIQUES AND THE SINGLE PLOT: 300 SQUARE
YARDS

CHAPTER 1   GROW IT YOURSELF   3

*The plan of the book; facts on allotments; gardening versus
agriculture*

CHAPTER 2   SOIL MANAGEMENT   9

*Soil texture; water; drainage; making a good garden loam;
making compost; lime; peat; chalk; organic fertilizers; the
fertilizer analysis*

CHAPTER 3   DIGGING AND SOWING   24

*Tools; object of digging; deep digging; a do and a don't; the
digging controversy; manuring; use of fertilizers; sowing seeds;
covering; a drill; hoes; pricking out; the nursery bed; hardening
off; planting out; pinching out; catch crops; rotation; mulch;
cloches; irrigation*

CHAPTER 4   VEGETABLE DICTIONARY: COMMON VEGETABLES
AND HERBS   38

*Broad beans; dwarf french beans; scarlet runner beans; beetroot;
brussels sprouts; cabbage; carrots; cauliflower/broccoli;
celery/celeriac, leeks, lettuces, marrows/courgettes,
onions/shallots; parsnips; peas; potatoes; radishes; spinach; sweet
corn; turnips/swedes; herbs for everyday and for enthusiasts*

CHAPTER 5   THE ANNUAL CYCLE IN THE 300 SQUARE YARD
PLOT   62

*Diagram for the plot; the way to continuous cropping; crop
storage; notes on the monthly charts; monthly charts; jobs for the
month and the time they take; returns and costs*

PART 2   THE DOUBLE PLOT: 600 SQUARE YARDS

CHAPTER 6   VEGETABLE DICTIONARY: EXOTIC AND
GREENHOUSE VEGETABLES   89

*Introduction; globe and jerusalem artichokes; asparagus;
cardoons; chard; chinese cabbage; cucumbers; endive/chicory;
fennel; kohl rabi; mustard and cress; mushrooms; asparagus;
peas; salsify; scorzonera; tomatoes. Greenhouse
crops   aubergines; green peppers; cucumbers; tomatoes; witloof*

CHAPTER 7   FRUIT DICTIONARY   103

*Introduction; apples; apricots; berries; cherries; red/white/black
currants; figs; gooseberries; grapes; melons; peaches/nectarines;
pears; plums; damsons; raspberries; rhubarb;
Summer/Autumn/alpine strawberries; fruit cages*

CHAPTER 8   THE ANNUAL CYCLE IN THE 600 SQUARE YARD
PLOT   135

*Alternative diagrams for the second half of the double plot; jobs
for each month; birds; wasps; time taken; returns and costs*

PART 3   THE PLOT X 4 OR QUARTER OF AN ACRE PLOT

CHAPTER 9   LAYOUT OF THE PLOT X 4   146

*Vegetables, fruit, wine, and tobacco; diagram of the plot; design
imperatives; notes on the diagram*

CHAPTER 10   THE VINEYARD   151

History; Phylloxera vastatrix; expected yields; preparation;
varieties; planting; disease control; pruning; cropping; ripening;
quantity and quality; the Law; books on wine making

CHAPTER 11   GROWING YOUR OWN TOBACCO   165

History; varieties; the Law; curing cooperatives; cultivation,
harvesting; pests and diseases

CHAPTER 12   GROWING NUTS   171

Filberts and cobnuts; untrained and trained bushes; walnuts;
chestnuts; almonds

HOW IMPORTANT IS ALL THIS?   177

APPENDIXES

  i   *Calculating irrigation requirements*   179

 ii   *Deep freezing vegetables*   188

iii   *Glass and plastic for protection*   189

iv   *Machines and sprayers*   192

Index   194

PREFACE

After demobilisation from the navy at the end of the War, I decided to try living off three acres of land which I first had to clear of scrub, while continuing to write my novels. It was, therefore, by the hardest kind of experience that I learned how to grow vegetables and fruit, on a subsistence plus sale of surplus basis. I have been gardening, making gardens and writing about gardens ever since.

I believe that any man or woman can very quickly learn to keep a household in vegetables and fruit by investing a few hours work a week. Until the last few years I am not sure that it was worth doing except for exercise. But there's no doubt at all that it is worth doing now.

In 1948 I planted a small vineyard of very early varieties of French and German wine-vines and found it possible to keep a household in wine. Since then, wine-drinking has become much commoner here than ever before; I have therefore included in this book an account of how to plant and care for a vineyard.

In the 1950s I added tobacco to the crops I was cultivating; I was not, in that case, an innovator, others had been before me. It has since become easier to have the tobacco you grow professionally cured. Owing to the Customs and Excise waiver of duty on tobacco grown for smoking by the grower and his family, the saving is substantial. I have, therefore, included an account of tobacco growing.

A final point: although I have suggested varieties of vegetables and fruits in certain cases, I have not done so as a rule. The number to choose from is enormous, and once you begin studying seedsmen's catalogues you will make your own choices; you will also get to know from experienced gardeners which varieties do best in your part of the country.

PART 1   BASIC TECHNIQUES AND THE SINGLE PLOT: 300 SQUARE YARDS

CHAPTER 1   GROW IT YOURSELF

The cultivation of vegetables and fruit by the amateur grower, in his private garden or rented allotment, has again become worthwhile, because of the enormous rise in the price of those commodities. There is also a long-term reason why it will be increasingly necessary to encourage the practice: there is now a world shortage of food and very little prospect of improving the position.

This book is devoted to a method, based on experience and long practice, of raising the maximum quantity of vegetables from a small plot, in this case 300 square yards, that is to say 10 rods, the standard allotment. This plot is treated as a basic unit for producing the household's vegetables and salads. Having dealt with that, I multiply it by 2 and go on to deal with growing your own fruits and an increased crop of vegetables. If then you multiply the plot by 3, you can add wine growing to the other activities and become self-supporting in wine. Finally, unit x 4 will enable you to add tobacco-growing and you become as near to being self-supporting in food, drink and smokes as you can be on less than quarter of an acre, and without going in for livestock.

By way of encouragement I propose to begin this book with some introductory dialogue touching the law, history and economics of the amateur grower's contribution to his own and to the national larder, as established by surveys and enquiries carried out by the Ministry of Agriculture, the Universities, and other institutions.

Q   How do I, who have no garden; or I, who do not want to spoil my flower garden, get an allotment?

A   By renting it from your local council authority.   By the Allotment Act of 1922 (modified by later Acts of Parliament) all local authorities are under a statutory obligation to provide allotment gardens for all suitable persons provided application is made by six registered electors or six rate payers residing in the district.

Q   What exactly is an allotment garden?

A   It is defined in the Act as '. . . an allotment not exceeding 40 poles in extent which is wholly or partly maintained by the occupier for the production of vegetable or fruit crops for consumption by himself and his family.'   So the maximum plot is quarter of an acre; in practice very few people want as much land as that, and the commonest allotment garden measures ten rods, that is to say 300 square yards.

Q   On what terms shall I get my allotment?

A   Allotment gardens are let to tenants on yearly agreements terminable by either party giving six months notice to the other.   Notices to quit must expire outside the cropping season, that is before 6 April or after 29 September.   The rent of a 300 square yard plot is about £2 a year.

Q   What quantity of food crops can I expect to harvest from a 300 square yard allotment, or from my private garden of about the same size?

A   In the middle of the 1950s the municipal authority of Keighley, Yorkshire, commissioned Mr T. L. Ashton to carry out a trial to establish the quantity and variety of crops which could be harvested from a 300 square yard allotment.   The result was as follows:

224 lbs of peas
 77 lbs of beans
 92 lbs of carrots
150 lbs of cauliflower
268 lbs of onions
525 lbs of cabbage
 94 lbs of beet
150 lbs of brussels sprouts

4

This represents a cropping rate of more than ten tons of food per acre.

Q Is there any significance in the choice of crops?

A Yes: it made possible an all-the-year-round succession. But other choices could have been made. There is one other thing: it would seem from the results of surveys that there are some crops with which the gardener does better than the farmer, and others with which the farmer does better than the gardener. In *The Land of Britain, Its Use and Misuse* (Longmans London, 1948), Professor Dudley Stamp published a list of crops comparing the average results obtained by gardeners and by farmers on land of comparable quality. Here is that list (figures in tons per acre):

Gardeners	Farmers	
7	6.9	of potatoes
3.5	3.7	broad beans
4	4.2	runner beans
9.4	11.5	beetroot
5.8	4.6	brocolli and cauliflower
3.2	2.9	brussels sprouts
9	10	cabbage
12	10.4	carrots
10.9	8.9	celery
8	8	leeks
6	6	lettuce
4.7	4.7	onions
11	8.9	parsnips
10.2	7.8	turnips

Q It would appear from these figures that the average gardener is getting 7.1 tons of food per acre, the average farmer only 6.3 tons of market-garden crops. Why is this?

A In the garden cultivation is intensive; on the farm it is extensive.

Q It would seem in that case that, where vegetables are concerned, the gardener on his small plot is a better food-producer than the farmer. Is he?

A Yes. By whatever standard the comparison is made and however carefully the figures are adjusted to ensure that the comparison is fair, that is true. In money terms the difference is even more striking than in terms of weight:

5

Wye College (London University) found that after all adjustments necessary to make the comparison meaningful, the gardener gets *three times* the farmer's crop per acre in cash value.

Q   What proportion of the household's food consumption can the amateur gardener expect to produce from 300 square yards of garden or allotment?

A   During World War II, a period comparable in terms of food shortage to our own, the proportion of the total food consumption of an average working-class, urban household which was home grown was not lower than 10% in any quarter of the year, and as high as 25% in the third quarter of every year.

Q   Will I save money by growing my own vegetables and fruit?

A   Yes, even if you load the cost of production with £1 an hour for your own time or that of anyone who helps you in the garden, for the obvious reason that no wholesaler's mark-up, no retailer's mark-up and no costs for carriage need be added to your production costs.   You can probably cut your annual greengrocer's bill by 75%.

Q   From all the above it would appear that the amateur gardener growing food crops is making a contribution to the national economy as well as helping himself.   Is he?

A   Yes, a surprisingly large one.   Remember that not all our vegetable, salad and hardy fruit is grown in Britain, much of it is imported.   As long ago as 1956 the import-saving contribution made to the national balance-sheet by the amateur food grower was about £50 million.   Today it could easily be of the order of £200 million.

Q   We hear a great deal about the harmful effects, in terms of food production, of letting more farm land be taken for housing estates.   Is this strictly true?

A   No, not if the houses on the estate have gardens in which the owners or tenants grow food.   It was clearly established by Wye College (see *The Garden Controversy* by Best and Ward, 1956) that where the gardens on a housing estate are cultivated for food crops, the loss of food caused by building is very surprisingly nil.   What may be lost are specifically agricultural (as against horticultural) crops, *eg* cereals, meat, milk etc.

Q   How much of his leisure must a man give up to cultivate 300 square yards of land efficiently?
A   Difficult question; the answer depends so much on the
age, temperament etc of the gardener.   Between 250 and
300 hours per year.
Q   Surely there must be variations in the quality of the
land from region to region which will have an effect on the
gardener's productivity?
A   Yes, that's true.   The gardener who has what is called
good garden loam, that is a mature topsoil which has been
manured and cultivated for years, has an easier time of it
and does better than the gardener starting on virgin soil or
clay.   On the other hand, the soil of a new housing estate
may be very good and fertile if the estate is on old farm
land.   But remember that a suitable routine of manuring
with compost which is not difficult to make, will soon
mature the soil.   We shall be dealing with that subject in
the body of the book.
Q   Will the kind of soil I garden on affect my choice of
crops?
A   Yes.   For example, you can't grow good carrots on
heavy clay.
Q   Can I cultivate an allotment garden rented from the
municipality under the terms of the Act of 1922, for profit?
A   No.   The right to an allotment garden is conditional on
the tenant cultivating that allotment garden for his subsistence and that of his household.   There is a legal difference
between an allotment garden, and an allotment, confused by
the fact that we commonly shorten allotment garden to
allotment.   An allotment, properly so-called, is more than
quarter of an acre and can be as much as 5 acres.   Terms
of tenure are not the same and will be found under Section
3 (7) of the 1922 Act.   A true allotment can be cultivated
for profit.

Q   What is the origin to the right to an allotment garden?
A   Going back far, the fact that much of the land of England belonged in common to the people of England until
they were robbed of it by the Acts of Enclosure.   Com-
moners were compensated by grants of small holdings but
as these, unlike common land, were alienable, the buying
and selling of land became legal.   But the sentiment that

every man has a right to a piece of land for his own and his family's subsistence, survived and prompted a series of Allotment Acts culminating in the Act of 1922.

Q You have referred to the 300 square yard plot. Is there any significance in that other than the fact that it is the commonest size of allotment?

A Yes, there is. I propose to base the whole of this book on it. We shall take the 300 square yard plot as the unit under discussion and try to show how to get the optimum result in food production from it and to make clear its limitations. Then, by multiplying the unit by 2, and later by 3 and 4, we shall show how the cropping plan can be enlarged and enriched and the cost in capital and labour of doing so. It is hoped that by this means the gardener/reader will be able, by division or multiplication as the case may be, easily to adapt the plan to fit his own garden which may be larger or smaller (see p. 62).

CHAPTER 2   SOIL MANAGEMENT

Notice to reader   If you know all you want to know about garden soil, compost, and fertilizers, skip this chapter.

The soil of your garden is in two layers, sub-soil and top-soil.   The sub-soil is composed almost wholly of mineral particles whose chemical and physical properties depend on the nature of the local bedrock.   The top-soil is composed of the same kind of mineral particles as the sub-soil but also of organic particles, the detritus of vegetation in various stages of decay down to that called humus, the penultimate stage before final breakdown into component mineral elements.   Unlike the sub-soil, moreover, the top-soil is more or less densely populated by animals living on the organic material, notably earthworms; and by bacteria which, by fixing atmospheric nitrogen in compounds with other elements, make it available to plants.

As salts of nitrogen are one of the three major plant foods, these bacteria, some of which also live in nodules on the roots of certain plants (notably the pea and bean family which includes clover), are the world's most important living creatures.   Without them there would be no green plants, and as all animals including man live directly or at one remove on green plants, no life on earth.   Not until the last century did a chemist achieve the feat performed by these bacteria and so make possible the manufacture of nitrogenous fertilizers.

The other two major plant foods are salts of potassium and salts of phosphorus.   All soils contain all three nutrient groups, but in some one or more may be present in insufficient quantity. Such deficiencies can be made good swiftly by the use of chemical fertilizers; or slowly by the use of organic manures.

Soils also contain a whole range of other elements which are necessary for plant health and growth. They include copper, iron, manganese, magnesium and others and they are collectively known as trace elements because only traces of each are found when a soil is analysed. Deficiencies of any of them are indicated by recognizable symptoms of plant ill health, and can be made good specifically, or by a routine of general manuring.

The commonest soil deficiency disease of green plants is chlorosis; the leaves are yellow instead of green, and the plant is debilitated. Chlorosis is less often caused by an actual deficiency of iron than by an excess of lime or chalk in the soil: calcium compounds combine with iron so readily that the plants cannot get at the supply they need. Fortunately plants vary in their power to overcome this difficulty and very few food plants belong to those families (notably *Ericaceae*, to which belong cranberries and their allies), which suffer from a disability in this respect.

Excessive calcium in the soil is indicated by exceptionally low soil acidity. The acid/alkali balance of a soil is expressed as its pH figure. To understand what pH stands for you have to be an electro-chemist; for our purpose it doesn't matter. On the pH scale, 7 is neutral, so that soils with a pH below 7 are acid, and those above 7, alkaline. Anything between 6 and 8 suits the whole range of food plants with some very unimportant exceptions. Excessive acidity is corrected by dressings of chalk or lime; excessive alkalinity is much more difficult to correct, but can be done in time by heavy dressings of acid peat and composts.

I give these few facts because it is useful to know why you are doing the things you will be doing. It is possible and in fact usual to be a good gardener getting excellent results without knowing any of this; and most British soils are more or less satisfactory media for growing food plants.

Soil texture

The deeper the layer of top-soil, the better. On most British land it is at least one spit deep, which means as deep as the blade of a digging spade or the tines of a digging fork are long. It can be much deeper but in practice gardeners regard the top spit as the top-soil and everything below it as sub-soil. Top-soil can also be shallower in which case a bit of hard work and manure will be required to improve it. Very roughly speaking, annual and perennial plants—the group to which a majority of vegetable and salad plants belong—exploit the top-soil, though putting some roots down below it; shrubs and trees, including most fruit plants, can exploit the sub-soil.

Of primary importance to the health and growth of plants is the texture of the soil, especially the top-soil. Unless it is open and crumbly root growth is inhibited and therefore so is the growth of the plant as a whole.

Where the mineral particles of a soil are relatively large, the soil is said to be sandy. Sandy soils are by nature open to water and air; but unless their organic content is high, these advantages become disadvantages, for such soils dry out in periods of drought, and plants suffer.

Where the mineral particles of a soil are very small they adhere together in a dense mass we call clay. Clay is a very good medium for plants provided, once again, that there is a high organic content, not otherwise. Where there is plenty of humus, the mineral particles are collected in tiny balls by the elctro-chemical action of natural resins, so that the soil has the desirable crumbly texture. As to chalk, see what I have to say on p. 20.

Soils, whether basically sand or basically clay, become 'good garden loam', then, where they have a high content of decaying organic matter: loam is dark in colour, crumbly and moist in texture, and it smells sweet. If your garden or allotment is on land which was formerly old pasture, then you will have a good loam. Old woodland soils have much the same good quality.

The manuring programme suggested is designed to make (and maintain) the soil of your garden into such a medium that it provides the best conditions for plant growth.

11

Soil water

Water is found in three places in soil. At a point below the surface is a level below which the soil is completely saturated with water, a sort of subterranean morass. That level which is very variable is known as the water table. Trees and shrubs and some other plants put down tap roots into it. In dry years the water table falls, and in wet periods it rises. Next, there is free water in the soil; that is water which shares, with air, the spaces between soil particles. It is not pure water, but a solution of nutrient mineral salts in water—*ie*, it is plant food. In drought conditions this water disappears, because, taken up by plants and transpired into the atmosphere, it is lost to the soil until rainfall replaces it. Finally, there is captive water, the water which forms a thin film round every soil particle or which permeates the spongy organic particles. Plants can draw off some of this water, (which is, again, a solution of mineral salts), but not all of it; even after they have died of thirst some of that captive water will still be there.

For plants to be healthy and to flourish, both air and water must be freely and easily accessible to their roots. These conditions occur where the soil has enough organic content to keep it both open and moist; so once again we come back to the importance of soil texture. The ideal water condition of a soil from the point of view of plant health and growth is known as the soil's 'field moisture capacity', which is defined as 'the moisture content of a soil when it is holding all the moisture it can against the force of gravity'. As an appendix to this book I give the method by which a soil can be maintained correctly at field capacity by controlled irrigation. I relegate this to an appendix because while I know that readers of this book have the intelligence, I do not believe that many people will have the means to use this technically sophisticated method. But I do not leave it out altogether because it does teach the gardener what exactly he is trying to do when he waters the garden, and gives him an ideal to aim at.

Drainage

Water in soil is one of those good things one can have too much of. If the soil is saturated, so that all the air is driven out of it, your plants die by drowning. Consequently, good drainage is essential: what we want is not water lying stagnant in the soil, but water moving continuously through it. There is rarely any problem of drainage on sandy soils, but on clay soils there may be. Water is often held up by a hard pan of clay sub-soil. The cure is to break that up by deep digging.

Most British soils are quite well drained because for centuries, since Roman times, farmers have been putting in land drains to run off surplus soil water into ditches whence it is fed into rivers. The amateur gardener is hardly likely to find himself with a drainage problem so difficult that the fault cannot be cured by deep-digging the sub-soil. If he does, if his garden needs land drains, then it is no job for an amateur and he will have to seek expert advice and help. On the sort of land let for allotments, the tenant is not likely to encounter this problem.

Having described what is meant by a 'good garden loam', the next step is to describe how to make and maintain it.

Making a good garden loam

An ecosystem is a natural congeries of plants, animals and insects which are mutually supporting each other in a life cycle both complex in detail, and magnificently simple in principle. (In what follows I have excluded the roles of animals and insects, and even of the bacteria on which the working of the system depends). In any ecosystem of wild plants, life is maintained by a recycling, *ad infinitum,* of plant tissue. The root of a plant draws from the soil nutrient salts in solution; its leaves draw from the atmosphere carbon dioxide. By means of the process called photosynthesis the sun's energy—light and heat—are used to combine these substances to form plant tissue. The plant grows, matures, flowers, produces seed. In due course—a few months in the case of annuals, up to four thousand years in the case of some trees—the plant dies, its tissues

13

decay, are attacked by soil animals and soil bacteria, and reduced to their elements which thus become available to another generation of plants. Even the water the plants need is recycled: drawn from the soil it is transpired into the atmosphere by the leaves as water vapour, to return, in due course, as rainfall. So the plants of a natural ecosystem *use* the raw materials of their tissues but do not *consume* them.

But in an artificial system such as a vegetable garden, something quite different happens. The bodies of the plants growing in it are not allowed to decay back into the soil; they are harvested and eaten, becoming part of our body tissues. And since we do not return to the top-soil either our dung, (excepting in China), or our dead bodies the raw materials of life are, from the point of view of our garden soil, not being merely *used;* they are being *consumed* (unless we are using treated sewage). If this process is continued for a certain number of seasons, the soil ceases to be able to support plant life; its fertility declines, its texture is ruined. To avoid this disaster the gardener or farmer must continuously restore deliberately what, in a wild environment, would be restored naturally. Hence the need for manures and fertilisers.

You can maintain soil texture and fertility by the use of organic manures alone, as, of course, all mankind did from the invention of manuring in the late Neolithic epoch, until the third quarter of the 19th century. The soils of England, parts of Wales and Lowland Scotland were not merely maintained but greatly improved by this process, especially during the era of 'High' farming in the 18th and 19th century.

You can maintain soil fertility by the use of chemical fertilizers alone, but not soil texture. Indeed the exclusive use of chemical fertilizers will hasten its deterioration. It was this malpractice which led to the great dust bowl disaster in Oklahoma in the 1920s; and the similar disaster in the Ukraine in the 1950s.

In that case, why use chemical fertilizers at all? Although the farmer must do so if he is to feed our overcrowded world, there is a good case for the gardener to avoid them. It does not, however, convince me: fertilizers are quick acting and give very good results provided that organic manuring is also maintained. See what I have to say about this on p. 22.

Organic manuring is done either with animal dung or with compost.

Making a compost bin

For a 300 square yard plot you will need (basic minimum) a pair of compost bins. To make them you will need, to begin with, 6 wooden posts, 3 x 3 in timber, 6 ft 6 in long, pointed at one end and treated with a copper preservative. Choose a site beside a path, for easy access, and hammer these posts into the ground, taking care to get them all quite vertical and parallel to each other, in the following pattern:

Next you need 110 square feet of ½ inch to 9 inch gauge wire, or a rigid plastic netting. Staple this to the posts˙to form a pair of open-fronted cages, like this:

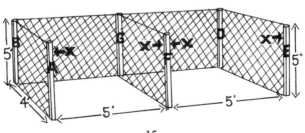

Now you need eight pieces of wood 1 x 1 in x 5 ft, treated with copper preservative. Nail these with 2 inch nails to the faces marked X of the posts A,F,E, like this:

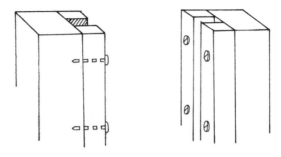

Finally you will need twenty 5 ft planks 6 x about ⅞ in which can be dropped, one at a time, into the slots shown in the above drawing, to close the front of the bins as the compost level rises. When closed the bins will look like this:

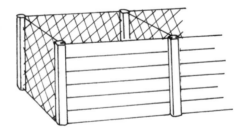

Old Chinese proverb: one picture is worth a thousand words.

Using the bins

METHOD 1 (Where farmyard or stable manure is available).
(1) Put garden weeds, dead leaves, kitchen waste, rags of cloth made of natural fibres, wastepaper unsuitable for

16

recycling, sawdust, grass mowings, tea leaves, coffee grounds, nettles, hedge clippings—in short any organic material whatsoever onto the floor of bin 1, treading it down lightly, and continuing until you have a layer 12 inches thick. This will be kept tidily in place by dropping two planks into the slots. Very coarse material such as cabbage stalks or twigs should first be chopped up with a spade.

(2) Now put a layer of farm or stable manure about six inches thick and dust the top with lime or ground chalk, and add an inch or so of ordinary garden soil. The object of the chalk or lime is to reduce excess acidity; the object of the soil is to innoculate the heap with earthworms or their capsules.

(3) Continue putting on organic waste till you have another layer 12 inches thick.

(4) Add another layer of farm of stable manure six inches thick and dust with lime and soil.

(5) Continue this alternation until the bin is full. Top off with stable manure and top dress with lime. You then begin with bin 2 in the hope that bin 1 will have been cleared by the time bin 2 is full.

In persistently wet weather, cover the bins with a sheet of polythene. In persistently dry weather, water the heap thoroughly with the hose twice a week and then cover with polythene to check loss of water by evaporation.

In my experience this is all you need to do. Real compost enthusiasts would have a third bin so that they can turn the heaps at 3 monthly intervals, top to bottom. This is hard work but it has two advantages; it ensures that fermentation temperatures rise so high several times that weed seeds are killed; and it ensures even decay all through the heap. I advise this but do not practice it.

METHOD 2 (Where no farm or stable manure is available).
Do as for method 1 but as soon as you have a twelve inch layer sprinkle the top quite liberally with sulphate of ammonia (from any good garden shop) and about a dozen handfuls of fine bone meal. Alternatively, you can use a balanced fertilizer such as Fison's 'Extra Yield' and, if you are lucky enough to have a wood fire in your house, you

17

can also use wood ashes (potash).   Add an inch of garden soil.

Each bin will yield approximately 100 cubic feet of compost and you should be able to make 200 cubic feet of the stuff every year.   This will keep the soil of a 300 yard plot in good condition.   For a larger garden you will need more bins.   I am assuming that you will also use small quantities of chemical fertilizer—see pp 20-23 below.

Well finished compost is a moist, crumbly, sweet-smelling, almost black substance differing from a rich, matured Christmas cake in that it is populated by young earthworms.

Warnings

Do not let compost making become a mania; the object is to grow crops, not to make compost.   Compost maniacs cover so much land with bins that there is no room to grow any food; and even have the household lavatories drained onto the heaps—ecologically sound but socially offensive.

Do not put into the bins any objects made of plastic or metal, any rags of cloth made of man-made fibres such as nylon: they are not, alas, biodegradable.   Nor is human or animal hair in under ten centuries.   Stock-pot bones and corks will take many decades to decay but will do no actual harm.   Even rags of wool, silk, cotton and linen dyed with modern dyes are troublesome and may have to be removed from the compost and re-composted.

With this pair of compost bins you can provide the material to put back into the 300 yard plot the essential substance of the crops you are going to take out of it.   To cheer you up, there are aspects of compost making which appeal to the imagination: when you put tea leaves and coffee grounds, orange peel and banana skins and avocado pear skins into your fermentation bin, you are gaining for your own garden a fraction of the fertility, conveniently packaged, from some tropical garden, transferring the soil capital of remote places to your own soil bank account.   It's an investment which cannot depreciate in value.

Lime

Garden or 'slaked' lime has considerable value on certain soils, none on others, and can be pernicious. Here is a rough and ready rule: if you garden on chalk or in one of the limestone regions, forget lime; if not, then you may need to know how to use it.

Garden lime $(Ca(HO)_2)$, neutralises acids in the soil. In other words it de-acidifies very sour or acid soils. Now, in acid soils which are also heavy (clay), the incidence of a troublesome disease of *Brassica* crops—cabbage, cauliflower, broccoli, brussels sprouts—is high. So the use of lime can prevent this disease (see below). Second point; while lime ties up iron compounds so that some plants have trouble in getting enough iron, it works the other way with potash, *releasing* it from compounds. Very few of our kitchen garden plants are likely to be stunted by iron deficiency but a great many can suffer from potash deficiency, so that on balance it is better to have enough lime in the vegetable garden soil than not enough, though the same amount of lime would kill, *eg*, your rhododendrons. Third: lime, like humus, causes the tiny particles of a clay soil to assemble in minute balls, and so tends to make it crumbly, and therefore a better rooting medium. Finally, since all plants require a small amount of the metal calcium, (as do all animals including man; it is the stuff of bone, teeth, fingernails, claws, seed shells, etc) and as the metallic element of lime is calcium, there must be some source of calcium in the soil if plants are to flourish.

Two more rules:

On acid soils, use lime in the kitchen and fruit garden at the rate of one ounce per square yard per annum.

On chalk or limestone soils do not use it at all.

Never use lime at the same time as you use uncomposted farmyard or stable manure; if you do you will get an excessive release of ammonia which can kill young plants and reduce soil fertility. Instead, add it to your compost heaps in the form of light dustings on each layer.

Lime is a good thing; but it is one of those good things which gardeners can easily have too much of. Very, very roughly, if your cabbages are stunted and have roots which look like a human hand deformed by severe arthritis—your soil badly needs liming. But it's better to find out first rather than wait for a failure. Garden shops sell a kit which enables you to discover the acid/alkali balance of your soil.

Peat

Granulated horticultural peat is a marvellous soil conditioner: it gives substance to sands and openness to clays; and it makes the soil very water retentive. But it should not be used on acid (low pH) soils because it is very acid itself. Its use on an effective scale in the open garden, *ie* not merely as a potting compost, is extremely expensive. If you do make use of it, *eg* because you cannot make enough compost, *never* use it dry; soak it first. Dry peat draws the moisture out of the surrounding soil and can hold an incredible quantity. It is possible to lower the pH of excessively chalky soils by the consistent and repeated use of very large quantities of peat. But the job is very expensive and, for the vegetable grower, not necessary.

One is always told that peat is useful only as a soil conditioner, being devoid of fertility. I find this very hard to believe since a number of plant genera, *Rhododendron* for example, will flourish in pure peat.

Chalk

People who garden on chalk are always grumbling about it. There's no excuse for this. The late Sir Frederick Stern made one of the most glorious gardens in Britain on the solid chalk of East Sussex. The secret is very deep digging to start with: the chalk sub-soil should be broken up to a depth of 2 feet. A daunting task but it need only be done once.

Organic fertilisers (as distinct from manures)

There are a number of fertilisers which come in easily manageable, dry, powdered form but which are not industrially synthesized and are organic. The most important of these are dried blood, bonemeal, and hoof-and-horn meal. Fishmeal is another, but it is neither as common nor as cheap as it used to be.

Dried blood is far too expensive to be used for anything but plants in pots. Neither bonemeal nor hoof-and-horn meal are cheap but they are used in very small quantities and are so long lasting in their effect that they are economical. Both release into the soil phosphates and also some nitrates, so that they are providing two out of the three major plant nutrients; they also provide some calcium.

Their action is faster in sandy soils than in clay soils, longer lasting in clay than in sand. The more finely the material is ground, the quicker acting it is and the shorter lived.

An annual dressing of the coarsely ground meal, (not the coarsest, however, which is in one inch lumps, but the stuff like pinhead oatmeal), at the rate of one ounce to the square yard is a sound investment. Dust it on evenly and hoe or rotovate it into the surface. If you don't, birds will eat it.

Chemical fertilisers

Nitrogen, essential to the life of all plants, is absorbed by them in the form of water-soluble nitrates. The principal supply of these is produced from decaying organic matter by the process called nitrification, the agents of that process being certain bacteria, notably the azobacters or azotobacters. This supply can be supplemented by using dressings of sulphate of ammonia, sodium nitrate, potassium nitrate; and nitro-chalk (on acid soils only). The use of these will produce quick, often spectacular, growth. *But* unless these fertilisers are used sparingly and are balanced by the other two elements, especially by phosphates, in the correct proportional quantities (see Advice below), growth will be rank, soft, and vulnerable to disease.

Potassium is a major constituent of all plant tissue. It is absorbed from the soil in the form of potassium salts which are collectively referred to as potash. Potash ripens and matures and hardens the tissue as nitrogen produces it. It is also primarily responsible for fruit and vegetable flavours, the colours of flowers and the ripening of seeds. Fertilisers in common use are Potassium chloride and Potassium sulphate. The ashes of all organic material, and therefore of any wood fire or garden bonfire, contain quite a lot of potash and should always be scattered on the soil of the garden.

Phosphorus, vital to all plants, is absorbed from the soil in the form of water-soluble phosphates. There are two major sources of these, mineral, *ie* phosphatic rocks; and 'bone phosphates'. A number of phosphatic rock fertilisers are available, the most valuable of which are, after processing, called superphosphates.

ADVICE if you want to use chemical fertilisers, and provided you also make use of compost there is no good reason why you shouldn't and several why you should, do not try to use them individually; you will get the balance wrong. Buy one of the proprietary 'balanced fertilisers' and then use it sparingly: about two ounces to the square yard in March, and one ounce in July, tilled into the surface soil. Remember that these fertilisers are quick-acting and ephemeral; a dressing does not last more than one season because what is not taken up by the plants is lost by leaching, the process whereby water carries these salts down through the soil and, ultimately, into the drainage system, often causing pollution of rivers. The chemical symbols for nitrogen, phosphorus and potassium are N, P and K. So these ready mixed balanced fertilisers are called NPK.

The fertiliser controversy

A great many gardeners, a small number of farmers and a lot of people who are neither, but are fussy about their food, believe that food grown without the use of chemical fertilisers is more wholesome than food grown with them. There is no evidence for this, it is simply a belief. Logically, it should be nonsense: chemically, there is, no difference between the product of bacterial nitrification and industrial nitrification, and potash and phosphates are potash and phosphates however you make them. But my own objection to chemical fertilisers in the garden is that they are, given sufficient organic manure correctly composted and used consistently, an unnecessary extravagance. Unfortunately it is not easy for the urban gardener to make enough compost or to get farmyard or stable manure. If you have strong feelings against chemical fertilisers, don't use them; you can do the job perfectly well without them provided you keep up a more generous routine of compost manuring than I have suggested. Compost making is certainly more socially meritorious than using fertilisers; it recycles waste, whereas the fertiliser industry is a huge consumer of scarce commodities.

Here, for those with plenty of land, more than they need for cultivation, is a way of getting the best of both worlds. Grow a patch of mixed nettles and Russian comfrey (from seed), stimulating very lush growth with chemical fertilisers which you do not use on the garden. In June, mow down the nettles and comfrey and use them on the compost heaps. Continue this process as a routine.

Soil analysis

If you are taking over a new garden or starting to make one on virgin land, your wisest course is to begin by having a soil analysis. If you join the Royal Horticultural Society (Vincent Square, London SW1) they will do this analysis for you. Also Suttons of Reading will do it without charge. Take samples of your top-soil from various parts of the garden or plot, and send them in. You will receive in return an analysis showing whether or not your soil is deficient in any of the major nutrients and if so how to correct the deficiency and also giving you the pH so that you know whether or not to use lime.

I am not saying that you need to do this: only that it is the wisest course, for it enables you to start right.

CHAPTER 3   DIGGING AND SOWING

In all the chapters which follow this one the reader will meet with terms which may not mean anything to him if he is not and never has, until now, been a gardener. He will also be told to do certain things which, again if he has never done any gardening, he will not know how to do.

This chapter is for him.

Tools

If you are cultivating a 300 square yard plot or less, rely on hand tools: a digging spade—and have the edge sharpened as if it were a knife; one large and one small digging fork; a draw hoe, a push hoe and a very narrow or 'onion hoe' (see p. 30); a rake; a wheelbarrow; a dibber (see p. 33); a garden line (see p. 30); a pair of secateurs; a large ball of garden string; one pointed trowel and one blunt-ended trowel.

When you buy these tools, take a lot of trouble, especially with the spade and forks, to get the size and weight right for you. And buy good ones; cheap tools are a waste of money.

If your garden is in the quarter-acre bracket or larger, even, perhaps, if you are going to cultivate a 600 square yard plot, then a small light-weight motor rotovator will pay for itself in three years of use (see Appendix iv).

There are, by the way, gardening tools and devices especially designed for people with physical disabilities. To find out about the help you can get if age, accident or infirmity have made you less able to cope than you used to be, write to Disabled Living Foundation, 346 Kensington High

Street, London W14. They sponsored research into ways of making gardening easier for you. There is also a book which will help you: *The Easy Path to Gardening*, published by *Readers Digest*.

As we shall see, digging is not invariably a necessary part of vegetable growing. On some soils it can be avoided.

Object of digging

The object of digging, as of ploughing, is manifold: it turns-in the remains of the last crop, weed seedlings, fallen leaves etc; it gets the soil into condition favourable to the rapid and healthy growth of plant roots, by improving aeration and drainage; and it puts the soil into a suitable condition for making a seed bed.

Instructions for digging the garden seem always to assume that, having cleared off crops in the late autumn, you can then dig the whole area and leave it open to the beneficent action of frost, until seed time in spring. If, however, you propose to follow the plan of this book or something like it, and you'll have wasted your money if you don't, conditions for that practice will never exist because almost the whole area will be under crops all the year round. You will, therefore, be digging in long narrow strips at various times of the year.

This is the way to dig a long, narrow, strip—let's say a yard wide and ten yards long.

(1) At one end of the strip dig a trench the width of the strip, one yard, as deep as the spade or the tines of the fork, and as wide as the spade. All measurements are approximate. Put the soil you remove into a barrow and wheel it to the other end of the strip and leave it there.

(2) Facing the trench and with your back to the other end of the strip, dig the top-soil forward into the trench, turning it over and breaking it up as you do so, and, retreating backwards a step at a time, continue to do this till you have reached the far end. You then have a trench left; fill it with the barrowload of soil. The job is done. If you're inexperienced, the result will look uneven. Even it up with the rake, standing not on the newly dug soil, but beside it.

25

Deep digging

Deep digging or 'trenching' may occasionally be necessary if you have a really heavy clay or chalk sub-soil which is apt to form an impermeable 'pan' and obstruct soil-drainage.

This time, instead of taking out a narrow trench at the starting end of the strip to be dug, take out a square yard of top-soil as deep as the spade, and barrow it to the other end of the row; tip the barrow beside the row if possible, not on it, or it will be in the way later. You are now faced with a square hole one spit deep, with the sub-soil exposed.

(1) Dig this up and turn it over to the depth of the fork tines, levelling by knocking it about with the fork.

(2) Put the next square yard of the strip's top-soil onto the broken up sub-soil.

(3) Repeat 1 and 2 till you reach the far end of the row, when you will fill the remaining hole with the top-soil taken from the starting end.

The whole strip will now be well above the level of the surrounding soil. Never mind that; it will soon sink again.

A do and a don't

Do, if you have never done any digging or never been shown how to dig properly, find an old gardener and get him to show you. Digging isn't difficult but there is a right way to do it, that is a way which will get the most work done for the smallest cost in fatigue, and yield the correct result. Inexperienced or uninstructed gardeners poke round at the soil in an unhappy fashion and exhaust themselves to small purpose. Once you've been shown how to do it—it will take you quarter of an hour to learn—you can do the work with a very pleasant, slow-swinging rhythm which produces a handsome piece of work and is good and not tiring exercise for the whole body.

Don't ever, on any account, get the layers of soil turned upside down, that is, don't bring the sub-soil to the top and bury the top-soil. Sub-soil is not as fertile as top-soil but, more important, it has the wrong texture for seedbed and for young roots.

The digging controversy

Some say do dig; others say don't.

The pro-diggers say that what has been good enough for their ancestors and has fed the human race for about seven thousand years, is good enough for them, and anyway it stands to reason . . . etc. . . . .

The anti-diggers say that digging is not necessary since, demonstrably, plants in nature grow well without it. And that in any case it may be harmful since it breaks up the delicate structure of a stable soil and so interferes with the millions of delicate capillary channels by which water moves vertically in the soil.

Both sides are right, excepting in one particular—they ignore the nature of the soil. What may be right for one kind of soil can be wrong for another.

My own rules, based on experience, are these: if you garden on medium to heavy clay or silt soils, dig; and, occasionally, say every third year, trench or double-dig. If you garden on light loamy clay or on sandy loam, dig if you enjoy it, but don't if you don't want to; it won't matter.

If you do not dig, then how do you keep the surface soil open and clean and prepare a seedbed? By hoeing, or if you have much land, rotovating, to a depth of 3 or 4 inches only.

Manuring

If you follow the plan of this book (and have read the second chapter) you will, from time to time throughout the year, be spreading compost from your bins, to a depth of about one inch, on top of the soil. And that is almost all you will have to do. But as old hands and gardening friends with their own ways will certainly tell you that that isn't good enough, I will go a little further into the subject.

Traditional practice is to dig manures into the soil; if you use raw manure, you have to bury it because it's so coarse that you cannot plant into it. What one did was to remove a trench of top-soil, put in manure, cover it with the soil from the next trench of top-soil, and so on. In a very large kitchen garden where areas of soil could be left to lie fallow,

27

this worked very well. But we are here concerned with intensive cultivation of a small plot of land. If you plant vegetables into a soil manured in that fashion, you will get carrots with more fingers than your hand has, potatoes whose tops are up to your waist but without any tubers, and brussels sprouts so rank in growth that the stems cannot support their own weight and they lie down as if they were drunk or tired out.

Do not bury your compost; spread it on the surface and let it become incorporated with the top few inches of soil in the course of ordinary, necessary tillage by light shallow forking, hoeing or rotovating. It is true that the derivatives of this material are needed lower down; but the earthworms will do that work for you, just as they will bring to the surface a certain amount of sub-soil with its valuable store of nutrient minerals which are either part of the stuff of the native bedrock or which have been leached by rainfall out of the top-soil.

What is the justification for this claim? Observation: in nature, nobody but the earthworms bury the material which makes humus, yet trees and shrubs and herbs flourish; and experience—it works.

So your manuring will be done like this: you have just cleared a strip of the crops which have been growing there and are about to sow or plant another crop. If you are a digger you dig it, then spread your compost on it and lightly fork or hoe it or rotovate it into the top few inches. If you're not a digger, you begin by spreading the compost and then fork or hoe or rotovate it into the surface.

Use of fertilisers

As well as a regular routine of feeding and conditioning the soil with compost, some help from small amounts of chemical fertilisers will be useful.

It is usual to suggest specific fertilisers for particular crops—for example, root crops need phosphates as a priority, whereas spinach can do with more nitrates, and so forth. I am not going to advocate this practice, for two reasons. The first is that very few amateur growers have either the time or the background knowledge to carry out highly specific fertiliser routines; the second, and more important, is that provided the soil is continuously fed with good compost and helped with a general dressing of fertilisers at certain intervals, there really is no need to be so fussy, for if the soil is sufficiently rich in all that plants require, each kind of vegetable is perfectly well able to find and use what it needs most.

I therefore suggest that as well as the continuous feeding with compost already advocated as basic, the cultivator of a 300 square yard vegetable garden should give the soil a fertiliser boost with a general, balanced, NPK fertiliser twice a year and then forget that fertilisers exist. These two dressings should be as follows:

First half of March You will need, for the 300 square yard plot, 50 lbs of balanced NPK fertiliser. Sprinkle it as evenly as you can over the whole surface of your 300 square yard garden, but try to avoid getting it on the leaves of growing crops. Then hoe or rotovate the whole garden as soon afterwards as you can.

First half of July Repeat the above but with half the quantity—25 lbs.

By the time this book is in the shops we shall be buying fertilisers in kilograms. 20 kgs will be sufficient for the first dressing and 10 kgs for the second.

Sowing seeds

The manner in which seeds are sown depends on their size. To demonstrate what I mean by this I will consider two extreme cases: a broad bean, which is, of course, the seed, measures about 2 x 1 x 0.5 cms. A lettuce seed is so small and light that there are about 20,000 in an ounce.

Large seeds, like broad beans, peas, scarlet runners, can be placed in the drill (see below) individually spaced out. Very small seeds cannot be handled like that: they have to be sprinkled into the drill so that, after germination, when the seedlings are up, they have to be thinned. Seeds of intermediate size such as radish, still cannot easily be handled singly, but are easier to plant thinly.

There is another difference: the depth at which seeds are planted is proportional to their size. Thus, for broad beans one makes a drill 2 inches deep; but for lettuce the depth would be only half an inch.

Pelleted seeds Some very small seeds, lettuce seeds for example, are sold in pelleted form. The seed is embedded in a pellet of material containing a small amount of fertiliser. This not only makes it of manageable size, but gives it a good start. But make absolutely sure that the pelleted seeds are fresh; some pelleting materials have given trouble and if the pellets are kept too long the seeds will not germinate.

Covering When the seed has been sown in a drill—see below—it must be covered with soil. Using the back of a rake gently draw soil into the drill until it is full and level with the general surface. Firm it gently by pressing the back of the rake down on the loose soil.

A drill A drill, for sowing seeds, is simply a more or less shallow, narrow depression drawn in the soil along a straight line.

First, put the garden line—a length of thin cord fastened at each end to a peg and at least 10 yards long—where you want to sow your row of seeds, making sure that it is parallel with the rows of other crops and quite taut. Then draw out the drill along the side of the line with a corner of your hoe blade, or a pointed stick, or your finger if you like.

It will be obvious that you cannot conveniently draw out drills in soil unless the top few inches of soil is soft, crumbly, not too wet and is finely divided. That is what is meant by the term *Seed-bed*. You get the soil into this condition in one of two ways. If you are a digger, you first dig over the strip to be planted, breaking down the clods of soil as you do so, and then, by criss-cross raking, get the soil broken down finer and finer until the top three or four inches is in seed bed condition and is, by the way, flat and level. That's important because otherwise rainfall water will be unevenly distributed and may even collect in puddles. The other way, that of the non-digger, is to hoe the top three or four inches and then rake it down to a fine tilth, a fine, crumbly layer of two or three inches.

Hoes There are several kinds. The swan neck draw hoe is so shaped that you draw it towards you through the soil surface, while with the Dutch hoe you use a thrusting action, shoving it away from you. Hoeing soil simply means breaking up its surface with one of these tools to a depth of anything from one to about four inches. This operation not only makes the surface workable and aerates it, but digs up or cuts off weeds.

Pricking out Seeds are often sown not in the place where their plants are to grow, but in trays or boxes under glass—in a frame or greenhouse, or a nursery bed (see Appendix iii on use of glass etc.).

When the seedlings appear and are large enough to handle, it is necessary to 'prick them out' either into other boxes or pots so that they have more room to develop, or, for the same reason, into a nursery bed.

This is an operation requiring dexterity, neat fingers, gentleness and patience. Let's suppose you have a box full of lettuce seedlings to be pricked out into bigger boxes or trays before the final stage of planting out. First fill the boxes into which the seedlings are to be pricked out, with fine compost of sifted soil, pressing it firm and levelling it with a block of wood. Next, using an old, blunt kitchen knife or a flat, wooden plant label, carefully dig up a cluster of lettuce seedlings, and separate them. You have decided to give them two inches each way in their new quarters: make a series of holes in the compost with a short thin stick or a pencil, two inches apart in straight lines. Into each hole drop the roots of a seedling and with your fingers gently press the soil all round it, to fill and close it, so that the seedling is firmly planted. Firm—yes; but be gentle, small seedlings are very fragile.

A nursery bed is a small bed of fine soil on which to raise, or into which to prick out seedling vegetable plants such as cabbage, brussels sprouts, cauliflowers, leeks etc. It will be convenient to have it near the garden shed and compost bins although it is not marked as such on the plan you will find on page 63. For supplying a 300 square yard plot it need not be very large but it is worth while taking trouble over.

Having chosen a site for it, deep-dig (trench) it, removing from the soil stones, shards, lumps of clay etc. If you want to be very thorough you can sift it, but it will be a considerable undertaking. Having completed the digging of an

31

area rather bigger than the 10 x 4 ft which is about what you need, mark out the rectangular bed carefully with string and pegs, and enclose it in rough planks about 7 in x 1 in stood on edge, nailing them together at the corners with 3 inch nails. Throw the top-soil from immediately outside this frame onto it. You will then have a raised bed of fine soil.

This should be fed from time to time with compost sifted onto the top; and once a year with 2 lbs of hoof-and-horn meal (finely ground), 2 lbs of superphosphate and 1 lb of powdered chalk, sprinkled on the surface and well raked in.

Hardening off When seedlings have been raised under glass, especially if some artificial heating has been used, they are tender and not well adapted for full and immediate exposure to outdoor conditions. If seedlings in this condition are planted directly into their permanent quarters from their boxes or trays, many will be lost. So, before being planted out, they must be 'hardened off'. You do this by moving their box out into the open air in the morning and back under glass at evening, for four or five days. And then leaving them out, still in their boxes, day and night for a week or more. They should then be ready for:

Planting out This simply means taking the seedlings which were pricked out earlier and which have now grown to manageable size, from their boxes or from the nursery bed, into the open ground. The tool for this is a garden trowel with a pointed end. Take the box of seedlings with you to the site. Dig the first hole in the row with the trowel; then, also with the trowel, dig a plant from the box carefully, so that the soil remains on its root. Transfer to the hole, firm the soil with your hands: and repeat ill the row is complete. Then, tidy the soil surface by very shallow hoeing or raking.

Pinching out a shoot or bud is precisely what is says it is. You simply nip the tip of the shoot out between finger and thumb. What is the object of this operation? There are several. Let's suppose that your broad bean plants have set a crop of beans and reached a suitable height but are still growing. If you now 'pinch out' the growing tip, you achieve two things. You deny the aphis called Black Fly its favourite place for attacking the plants; and you

32

divert the plant's energy from growing into swelling the beans. By pinching out the small side shoots which develop on tomato plants, you prevent the growth of unwanted branches and keep all the plant's energy going into fruit production. And so on.

A *dibber* (or dibbler) is a tool for making neat holes in the ground about 1½ to 2 inches in diameter and up to about 10 inches deep. It has many uses, *eg* for planting leeks, sometimes for planting potatoes, often for planting cabbage and others of the cabbage family. It has a short wooden shaft, a handle like a spade handle, and a steel point. One can manage without it, but it's worth buying one.

Catchcrops

Radishes, spinach, lettuce in summer, turnips and carrots for pulling young, reach the harvesting stage very quickly. Therefore they can be raised between rows of longer term crops without much inconvenience. For example, you can raise and harvest a crop of radishes on the ridges of soil beside a celery row, before the soil is needed for earthing-up the celery.

Rotation

No vegetable takes from the soil the same quantity of each nutriment as any other kind of vegetable. For example, root crops are greedy consumers of phosphates, the cabbage tribe use a lot of nitrates, but peas leave the soil richer in nitrates than they found it. It is, therefore, a good idea to avoid planting the same crop or kind of crop in the same station in successive seasons; and to try to follow certain crops with different ones whose requirements in the matter of nutrients are not quite the same. Thus, peas should follow celery; cabbages and brussels sprouts and cauliflowers should follow onions which should then be followed by cabbages etc again. This is known as Rotation Cropping, and it has a secondary as well as its primary purpose. Most diseases and pests of vegetables are specific to a single family or even genus of plants. If, then, a strip of ground carries the spores or eggs or an organism parasitic on, *eg,* peas and beans, because peas have been grown there, and you sow beans on it, they will be attacked. But if you plant cabbage or potatoes there, the parasite cannot hurt them.

It should be said, however, that it is not easy to practise rotation systematically on a 300 square yard plot in continuous all the year round cultivation; what is more, it is not necessary where a routine of continuous composting is followed because the compost (and fertilisers) are continuously replacing the nutrients taken out of the soil by your crops.

The thing to do is to avoid growing the same crop or kind of crop in the same place year after year but not, so long as you are using compost, manure and fertiliser, to make rotation into a fetish.

Mulch

A mulch is a layer of material, usually organic, laid on the surface of the soil round plants, and whose principal purpose is to retain soil moisture by checking evaporation of water from the soil by the sun.

A mulch is often simply compost or raw farmyard manure and by ultimately rotting into the soil, also acts as a manure. But all kinds of material can be used: straw, cotton waste, spent hops, oil seed wastes, rags, tea leaves, coffee grounds, sawdust, the emptyings of vacuum cleaners etc. These, and similar materials, being what is called biodegradable, will ultimately rot into and so enrich the soil.

Some mulches, however, may be simply to retain soil humidity or even enhance it, and will not actually manure it. An example of this is mulching with pebbles which not only check evaporation from the soil surface, but, by condensing dew at night and filtering the water down to the soil, actually distil water for the plants. A mulch of that kind cannot conveniently be used in the vegetable garden, but it can be used round fruit trees in the drier parts of Britain.

In the kitchen garden the crop most likely to benefit from a mulch of compost is the late summer/early autumn pea crop.

Cloches

These are glass or transparent plastic contraptions for covering rows of plants thus providing them with protection from cold at night and giving them a higher temperature in the daytime. Their use gives you earlier crops of such salads as lettuces, and enables you to grow crops which cannot be grown without them, such as greenhouse cucumbers and melons. (See also Appendix iii.)

Originally glass cloches were shaped like a very large bell with a handle for lifting—whence the name, *cloche* is French for bell. Modern glass cloches consist of rigid wire chassis holding sheets of glass in place, and are of various shapes, either flat topped or barn shaped. They have some disadvantages: breakages are apt to be expensive, they are rather heavy, and they cost more than plastic cloches. But, at least in my experience, they are far more satisfactory than plastic cloches. Most crops do better under them, they are a much better protection against frost, and if you're careful when handling them they have a long life. I have tried many kinds and the most manageable, as it is also the most ingeniously designed, is the Chase cloche. Each one is 2 feet long, so for a 10 yard row you would need 15.

Plastic cloches are cheaper and lighter; also, humidity under them is higher, for some reason, than under glass cloches. They give little protection against frost, however, and unless very firmly anchored they very easily blow away in windy weather. They don't last long, either. The high humidity they afford is useful with some crops, *e.g.*, cucumbers. The plastic tunnel is the most recent form of cloche, but it is rather tiresome to manage (see p. 191).

The novice gardener should do without cloches until he has had two seasons' experience of plant behaviour. After that he should consider having a couple of rows.

Irrigation—which is watering

It is difficult to get consistently good results from a vegetable garden unless provision is made for watering. There is an illusion that the one thing Britain has enough of is rain. Perhaps it has, but a lot of it comes at the wrong time, it is unevenly distributed, and, owing to the inability

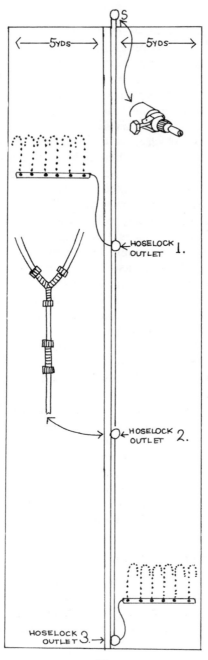

S

5 YDS   5 YDS

HOSELOCK OUTLET 1.

HOSELOCK OUTLET 2.

HOSELOCK OUTLET 3.

36

of successive governments to grasp the fact that water is the most valuable of all the raw materials of agriculture and industry, and the principal domestic necessity, most of our rainfall is wasted.

If you are the owner of your garden, ask the local water authority to put in a standpipe for watering the garden. On allotments there should be a standpipe you can use.

The easiest way to manage irrigation is as follows.

(1) Buy enough plastic hosepipe ½ inch gauge—to reach from the standpipe to your vegetable garden; there's your source of supply and I'll call it Point S.

(2) Buy enough of the same hose to reach from Point S the whole way down the middle of the 30 x 10 plot—*ie* 30 yards. If your vegetable garden is some other shape then you need enough to reach down one of its longest sides.

(3) You will now need certain devices which make every man his own plumber, called 'Hozelock' and sold in garden shops, garden centres and hardware stores. These will enable you, by cutting hose no. 2 into 10 yard lengths, to make an irrigation system which looks like the one on p. 36.

(4) Finally, you will need another short length of hose and a 5 yard length of sprinkler hose which is made of plastic, flat not round, pierced with hundreds of minute holes on one side. By laying the sprinkler hose between rows of crops and connecting it to any of the outlets marked 0 in the drawing, you can give an artificial rain to two rows of crops at a time, while getting on with other work.

CHAPTER 4   VEGETABLE DICTIONARY:

COMMON VEGETABLES AND HERBS

I include here only the most essential vegetables, leaving out the more de luxe kinds, and also leaving out those salad crops like tomatoes and cucumber which are, botanically, fruits.   These will be found in Chapter 6 where the subject is not so much intensive as expansive horticulture.

The intensive cultivation of a vegetable garden is a cyclical process, planting and preparation continuing throughout the year.   In Chapter 5 I shall be suggesting ways of managing that process.   Anyone who feels happier seeing the whole first, rather than the parts, should go on to that chapter now and then come back to this one.   I personally think it will be best first of all to say what is necessary about the cultivation of each of the principal kinds of vegetables and herbs, and only thereafter to demonstrate how to fit each operation into the pattern which forms the growers' year.   In other words, to provide the reader with a vegetable dictionary to which he can refer when it comes to the round-the-year working of the 300 square yard garden.

Bean, *Broad*   Can be sown in open ground from November until April inclusive, in mild dry weather.   November planting usually yields an earlier crop.   Single rows 18 to 20 inches apart; drill 2 to 3 inches deep.   Sow seed at 4 inch intervals and later thin to 8 inch intervals by pulling out alternate seedlings when the plants are 4 or 5 inches tall.   The reason for this is to allow for failures and accidents.   When sowing in November choose dwarf long pod varieties which stand up best to bad weather.   For March/April sowing, choose taller long pod varieties, as they bear a heavier crop.

Keep the rows clear of weeds at all times by light hoeing as required. Soon after flowering the young pods will appear—*ie* the crop has 'set'. When this process is nearly complete, pinch out the growing tips of the plants. This will reduce the danger of attack by Black Fly (see below).

Pests and diseases   Although broad beans *may* suffer from a number of pests and diseases, in ordinary practice the only one you need worry about is Black Fly whose scientific name is *Aphis fabae*. You cannot possibly mistake this tiresome creature: you will see on the soft stem at the growing tip of the plant dense clusters of minute black insects, and if they are not dealt with at once they'll spread with tremendous speed. Spray each plant thoroughly with an aphis killer—*eg* Malathion. You buy this at your garden shop and follow mixing and other instructions very carefully. Keep an eye on the plants; you may need to spray more than once.

Bean, *Dwarf French*   Otherwise called Kidney Beans because of their shape. These are grown from seed. They are dwarf, bushy, plants requiring no support. You can eat either the green pods; or, letting the beans ripen, the dried beans themselves, as 'haricot' beans. Seeds can be sown from the last week in April till the first week in July inclusive. Rows about 20 inches apart. Plants about 9 inches apart in the rows. But sow seeds 3 inches apart to allow for failures: when the plants are growing well you can thin to 9 inch intervals by pulling out the surplus plants. Irrigate in dry weather and if you want continuous supplies, be sure to pick the pods *before* the beans inside start to swell, because once that happens flowering will cease. Keep the rows free from weeds by hoeing, as required.

Pests and diseases   See Bean, Scarlet Runner.

Bean, *Scarlet Runner*   This is the best of the beans eaten as a green pod. It is a tall and fast-growing twining plant. You will therefore need supports and the simplest you can use are still ordinary tall stakes or poles. These should be from one inch to an inch and a half in diameter, about 7 feet long (longer = better) and pointed at one end.

Begin by fixing these in position: lay out two garden lines

a yard or so apart, and at 18 inch intervals stick the poles firmly into the ground so that those of one row slope towards those of the other and cross three inches from the top. (See diagram above). Bind and tie each pair of poles together at the crossing point. You will then have a 'V' at the top of each pair of poles. Into these 'Vs' lay bamboo canes, tying them in place, to form a continuous perch from end to end of the structure. Make all very firm; it has got to stand up to wind when carrying a great weight and volume of vegetation.

In the first weeks of May bury three seeds of scarlet runner two inches deep round the foot of each pole. When the seedlings appear, thin to one plant per pole. Each plant will climb a pole by twining and in due course the whole structure will be covered. Irrigate in dry weather. Keep weeds down by hoeing. Gather the pods while they are still flat, before the beans inside begin to swell. If you don't do this regularly, flowering will stop and you'll get no more pods.

If they do get away from you, let them develop fully on the plant and use as haricot beans. If you want scarlet runners until autumn, make a second sowing in the first week in June.

40

Pests and diseases Both dwarf and runner beans can be attacked by pests and diseases but, if clean fresh seed is used, disease can be discounted. Occasionally the plants are attacked by a fly whose grubs eat the roots. Since DDT was made illegal there's not much you can do about it; but, in my experience, it's extremely rare, so forget it.

Beetroot Beetroot is grown from seed sown in April/May for summer crops and in July for winter crops. The soil for beet seed should be raked very fine. Drills should be only 1 inch deep. Sow the seed thinly by sprinkling into the bottom of the drill. When the seedlings are about an inch tall, go along the rows with a hoe and hoe gaps in it, so that each group of 3 or 4 seedlings is separated by three or four inches. When the seedlings are about 2 inches tall, thin the groups by hand until you have a row of single seedlings six inches apart. Keep clear of weeds by light hoeing. Harvest as needed.

Pests and diseases Several, but with clean cultivation and the use of only fully rotted, fine, compost they rarely recur. If they do, they will not destroy the whole crop and in any case they are very difficult to control. Don't worry.

Broccoli See *Cauliflower*

Broccoli, *Sprouting* See *Cauliflower*

Brussels sprouts If you have a glass or plastic frame for raising your own seedlings, sow the seed in it in late February. Prick out into a nursery bed when the seedlings are 2 inches tall. And in the last week of May transplant them to their rows in the main garden, 30 inches apart in the rows. As the rows in our basic plot (see Chapter 5) are just over 20 inches apart which is not quite enough for brussels sprouts, if you plant several rows, as you should, don't do it like this

     •   •   •   •   •   •

     •   •   •   •   •   •

but like this   •   •   •   •   •

     •   •   •   •

   •   •   •   •   •

If, when you do this transplanting, the soil is moist and the weather showery, good: if the soil is rather dry and there is no rain in prospect, then the plants should be 'puddled' in. Make a hole with your dibber; drop the root and not quite all the stem of the plant into it; fill the hole with water from a watering can without a 'rose' or sprinkler; and tread the earth firm round it.

Like all *Brassica* species, (cabbage, brussels sprouts, cauliflower, kale etc,) brussels sprouts should be planted very firmly. When you have the young plant's root in the hole, tread the earth into it with your heel, putting all your weight on it, (I don't mean you have to stamp *on* the plant, but just beside it). Keep down weeds by shallow hoeing.

As you know—or maybe you don't if you're new to vegetable growing—brussels sprouts produce a long stem with leaves all the way up, the sprouts growing in the axils of the leaf stalks. In due course, the leaves begin to die; they turn yellow. When that happens, remove them. Old gardeners will tell you to nip out the tops of the plants to encourage the sprouts to grow. Don't do it; keep the tops until the sprouts have been picked; you can then pick and eat them.

When hoeing out weeds in the brussels sprouts rows, keep the hoeing very shallow, to the top inch of soil. If brussels sprouts are grown in loose soil, the sprouts are loose; the firmer the soil, the firmer the sprouts. Don't ask me why—I've no idea, but it is so.

Diseases and pests: See *Cabbage.*

Cabbage, *Spring* The seed should be sown in July or August, in a nursery bed; thinned when the seedlings are 2 inches tall, and transplanted into their rows in the garden when they are about 8 or 9 inches tall, in September/October. The drill for the seed should be about one inch deep. The cabbages should be spaced 12 inches apart in rows 20 inches apart. Plant by dibbing and if the soil is dry, puddle in the plants and make them firm with your heel. The firmer the ground the better will be your cabbage hearts. Keep clear of weeds by shallow hoeing.

Cabbage, *Summer and Autumn* As for Spring cabbage, but a succession of small sowings should be made in March,

April and May and transplanting into the garden rows in May, June and July. By this means you will have cabbage to follow the Spring supply until the end of October.

Cabbage, *Winter*   As for Spring and Summer cabbage, but the seed should be sown in May/June, transplanting in July, for cutting November, December and January.

Cabbage, *Savoy*   This is the hardiest cabbage and should be grown to make sure of a supply in very hard winters.   Grow as for the other cabbages, but the seeds should be sown in June, the transplanting done in August.   You will be able to cut Savoy cabbages from October until the end of March.
Pests and diseases   The worst pest of cabbages is the Cabbage White Butterfly whose caterpillars live on cabbage.   They can be picked off by hand and drowned; or the cabbages can be dusted with Derris powder.   Club Root disease may occur on acid or sour clays.   Once it occurs it cannot be cured, but it can be prevented in the future by dressing the soil with lime at the rate of 15 kilograms per 30 square yards, hoed in.

Carrots   It is essential that the soil where you are going to grow carrots be forked, hoed and raked to a very fine tilth four inches deep, to start with.   Make the drills less than an inch deep and they *need* not be more than 12 inches apart.   The thinner you can manage to sow the seed, the less thinning of seedlings you will have to do.   For an early crop choose one of the stump rooted varieties and sow the seed early in March.   Do the first thinning, leaving the little plants 2 inches apart, as soon as the seedlings are big enough to handle.   Then let them grow to just usable size so that the thinnings can be eaten.   And thin to 4 inches apart.   For later crops, make successional sowings in April, May, June and July.   Unless your land is very heavy, you can use the long or intermediate varieties for these.   Needless to say the rows should be kept free of weeds by hoeing.
Pests and diseases   Carrots suffer from several diseases but in good soil cleanly cultivated their incidence is rare and need not worry you.   The only really troublesome pest is the Carrot Fly.   There is not much you can do about it if you're unlucky enough to suffer an attack.   Don't leave

43

carrot thinnings or carrot foliage which has been cut off when harvesting, anywhere near the rows; it attracts the female flies who are the real villains, because it's the maggots which hatch from their eggs which attack your carrots.

Cauliflower It has become usual to call the cauliflowers you eat in summer by this name, and call Winter Cauliflower Broccoli. They are simply varieties of the same plant. Cultivation is exactly as for cabbage, so please refer to that. Seed for summer cauliflower, to be harvested July/September, should be sown in March, and the transplanting done May/June. Seed for the autumn supply should be sown April/May for June/July transplanting. Successional sowings in April and May of the winter varieties (Broccoli), with transplantings in June and July, can give you supplies throughout the winter. **Sprouting Broccoli** seed should be sown successively in April and May for transplanting in June and July and harvesting from as early as September to as late as March.

The cauliflowers grown in Britain are always white, but in Italy there are pink, green and purple varieties.

Pests and diseases See *Cabbage*.

Celery There are three kinds of Celery, all grown from seed: trench-grown celery; green or self-blanching celery; and turnip-rooted celery or celeriac. We'll begin with trench-grown celery, which, if well grown, is still the best.

Sow the seed as thinly as you can in a tray of soil, under glass, in March. In April prick out as many plants as you are going to need into deeper trays, or wooden boxes, 3 inches apart, and as soon as they are growing well again, move into the open.

Trenches should be prepared in May. The trench should be as wide and as deep as the blade of your spade. Put the soil you take out along the edges of the trench, on both sides, as you go. Trenches should be 40 inches apart.

Now put 3 or 4 inches of mature compost into the bottom of the trenches and lightly fork it in. If this work is completed at the end of May and weather is dry, flood the trenches with water and leave them for a week or ten days. Then, early in June, transplant the celery plants into the trenches, 12 inches apart. Irrigate if the weather remains dry and keep free from weeds—by hand weeding or careful hoeing.

When the plants are about 15 inches tall, the process of earthing up, for blanching, should begin. Some gardeners tie a tube of paper round each plant to keep the earth out, but it is not really necessary. Raffia ties or rubber bands can be used to pull each plant into a tight, closed bundle of stems and keep the earth out of them. Then rake earth into the trenches a little at a time at intervals of two weeks until finally only the leafy, green tops of the plants are above the surface. The celery plants will continue to grow. August, earth them up again. And finally, late in September, rake earth up into a ridge on both sides, so that only the leaves are showing along the top of the ridge. Pat this ridge firm with a spade, so that rain is thrown off. You can begin to harvest the celery early in November but it will usually last until February.

For green or self-blanching celery no trenches are needed, it is grown on the surface like any other crop. Sow the seeds and do the transplanting in exactly the same way as for the trench-grown celery.

The seeds of celeriac are also sown at the same time and pricking out and transplanting done in the same way. No trenches are needed—grow it on the flat like green celery. Plant about 9 inches apart in rows 20 inches apart.

Pests and diseases Provided you buy seed from a reliable seedsman, you need not worry about diseases of celery. The only pest at all likely to be troublesome is Celery Fly: it lays its eggs on the leaves and the maggots mine into the leaves and cause blisters. Pick off and burn any mined leaves you notice when inspecting your celery or celeriac plants.

Leeks Sow the seeds in a shallow drill, thinly if you can, in the nursery bed in March. Excepting for weeding and watering as necessary, you need do nothing else until June. The seedlings will be ready for planting which you will do as follows. Mark the row with your garden line. You'll need a bundle of leek seedlings, a dibber at least a foot long and over an inch in diameter, and a watering can without sprinkler-rose. Make holes 9 or 10 inches

45

deep with the dibber at 9 inch intervals along the line. The rows should be 20 inches apart. Drop a leek seedling, root downwards, into the hole. Now fill the hole with water. Don't worry if the leek seedling disappears from sight; it'll soon pop up again. Don't fill the holes in: rain and the hoe when you are hoeing to keep the weeds down, will slowly, as the leeks grow, crumble soil into the holes.

This method ensures at least nine inches of blanched leek. But the leeks will, of course, grow well above the surface of the soil, so from time to time you should rake soil towards the leeks, from both sides, to form a ridge so that blanching is carried higher and higher all the time. This will give you a crop in December, January and February and March.

Pests and diseases Diseases: none you need worry about. There is one pest—the Leek Moth, whose small caterpillars mine the leaves. It is not common in Britain. It does not affect the blanched part of the leeks. I should forget it.

Lettuce There are three forms of lettuce; the common cabbage-shaped or 'French' lettuce; the tall Cos lettuce; and the 'Winter Density' group which is half way between the two in shape.

Here's a suggested lettuce programme. February: sow seeds of variety May King under glass and transplant to garden in early April.

Sow seeds of May King in the open in March, April and May, for succession.

Sow seeds of Sugar Cos in May, for summer crop, with a sowing for succession in June.

Sow seeds of Winter Density in July for early winter crop.

Sow seeds of Arctic King in early August for all-winter crop.

Lettuce seeds should be sown thinly in a drill less than an inch deep—½ inch is enough—in fine tilled soil. As the germination is always good, the thinning of lettuce seedlings is troublesome and tedious. I therefore suggest that in the case of this crop, you use pelleted seeds which are easy to space out evenly. The plants should, after thinning, be from 8 to 10 inches apart in rows 20 inches apart.

Lettuce should always be grown fast. Consequently they should be kept well watered in dry weather. In my experience Cos lettuces do not do well excepting during the warmest months of the year. And winter lettuce does much better if cloched. Lettuce rows must be lightly hoed regularly so that no weeds can grow. If you do this, then you need not worry about the pests and diseases of lettuce. They are rarely troublesome and in really clean cultivation, almost never.

Marrow There are both trailing varieties and bush varieties. Bush varieties are more manageable among other crops and should be preferred for our 300 square yard intensive garden.

Plant the seeds one per pot in small pots of John Innes compost at the end of April, and keep the pots, adequately watered under glass. The seeds may need extra warmth to germinate well, and you can most easily arrange for this by keeping the pots on a window sill indoors until the seedlings have two leaves each. Then put them out of doors still in their pots, and keep them under glass at night, for a week or ten days, but exposed in the daytime. Then leave them for a few days fully exposed night and day.

The plants can then be planted out about 20 inches apart in rows 20 inches apart. If you do have more than one row don't plant like this

```
 •   •   •   •   •   •   •

 •   •   •   •   •   •   •
```

but like this

```
   •   •   •   •   •   •   •

   •   •   •   •   •   •   •
```

If the marrows are cut young and small and treated as courgettes, they will go on bearing for a long time but if allowed to grow big and ripen they will not taste as good and the plants will stop bearing.

Pests and diseases None to worry about.

47

Onions are grown either from seed or from small bulbs called 'sets'. Here is a good onion programme.

In March, as soon as the soil is dry and crumbly enough to make a good tilth possible, rake the area chosen very thoroughly to produce a really fine seed bed. Now draw out very shallow (½ inch) drills, 12 inches apart for as many rows as you want. (See Chapter 3). Sow the onion seed thinly, cover it with soil and, if the soil is not too wet, tread the rows to firm them.

When the seedlings appear wait till they are about 1 inch tall and, using a very narrow hoe, hoe out some of them so that instead of a continuous row you have a row of groups with the gaps between the groups of seedlings, and the group of seedlings themselves, being 2 inches. Now wait until the seedlings are about 2 inches tall and thin each group, leaving four onion plants in each. The thinnings, though very small, can be used in a salad. Now wait again until the onions are the size of spring onions and thin again, using the thinnings for salad and leaving the onions 4 to 6 inches apart in the rows.

Keep the earth between the plants and the row lightly hoed to keep weeds down. Irrigate only in sustained dry weather—it's easy to over-water onions.

Onion sets You buy these from garden shops in March and April. They are little onions about the size of a new penny or two-penny piece. Prepare the ground as for seed and stick one little bulb into the soil at 4 inch intervals along the line, being careful not to get them upside down and not to bury them entirely. Hoe and weed as usual.

Seeds or sets? Decide how many rows of onions you want and plant half with seed and half with sets.

In mid August the leaves of the onions will begin to flag and turn yellow. Bend them over so that they lie down. Wait another month and, on a fine day, lift them, knock off the earth, and lay them somewhere to dry. As soon as they are dried, they can be stored for use in some cool, dry place.

Also in September make a sowing of onions exactly as in March and give them the same attention. This will give you spring onions very early, and a crop of very large ones in August. (For *Shallots* see p. 52)

Pests and diseases: None to worry about.

Parsnip Sow the seeds in late March, in shallow drills in a fine tilth. There are two ways of doing this, either in a continuous row or in groups of five or six seeds at 10 inch intervals along the line. Try the latter method. Rows should be 20 inches apart. When the seedlings are 2 or 3 inches tall, pull out all but one of each group. Keep the rows free of weeds by hoeing. You can start harvesting in October and continue right through the winter.

Pests and diseases: None to worry about.

Pea There are dwarf varieties and tall varieties. The dwarfs are easier to manage and best for winter conditions. The tall peas bear heavier crops of superior quality. I suggest dwarfs for an early crop and a tall variety for the main crops. Three varieties I suggest are, for the earliest crop Little Marvel, for the next, Early Award, and for the later main crop, Onward.

It is not unusual to make a first sowing of early peas in November but very little if anything is gained by this. The first sowing should be made in February in any dry, fine spell when the soil is workable. Drills for peas should be about 2 inches deep and the seed-peas planted at 1 inch intervals. (No thinning is necessary). The seeds should then be covered and the soil firmed over them.

Here is a programme of sowings which will give you crops from early June to early October:

About February 15 Sow Little Marvel.

About March 15 Sow Little Marvel, Early Award, Onward.

As soon as the March 15 sowings germinate and the seedlings show above the soil, put in another sowing of Onward. And if you want peas until October, put in a fresh sowing each time the last one shows its seedlings above the ground. The reason for planting all three varieties at the same time on 15 March (or thereabouts) is that they will give a succession of crops, since earlies mature faster than second earlies, and second earlies faster than maincrop peas.

The Early Award peas will need peasticks—which are simply small, twiggy branches of small trees, stuck into the ground on both sides of the row and 2 feet tall; the main-crop Onward peas will need 3 foot peasticks.

The late Spring and early Summer rows will simply need weeding and hoeing. But late summer and autumn peas are very liable to suffer from mildew; they don't really like the drier soil of that season. Irrigation helps and it is also wise to give them a mulch to retain moisture.

Pests and diseases Peas have their pests and diseases but none, barring mildew, which need worry you or which require treatments, excepting birds and mice. Several species of birds will pull up and eat the seeds and seedlings when the young plants are about an inch above the ground; and mice dig up and eat the seed-peas. Later in this book I shall have something to say about the advantages of cover-ing parts of the garden with a netting 'cage' (p.134). In default of that, however, the pea-rows should be protected against birds either by pea-guard netting or by sticking short sticks into the soil on both sides of each row and weaving a criss-cross of black cotton which the birds seem to distrust as a trap.

Something must also be done to discourage mice. Before sowing the seed-peas, make a thin paste of red lead, (from hardware shop) stirred into paraffin and then stir the seed-peas about in it till they are well coated with the paste. This will keep the mice off.

Potatoes are grown from tubers known as 'seed' potatoes which are not, of course, seeds but simply small potatoes. Since it is very important to have disease-free seed-potatoes, buy them from a reliable source. I can give no advice on variety for it depends on whether you like white, yellow or red kinds, floury or otherwise. Also on which varieties are best in your neighbourhood, which you can find out by enquiry. You will need 2 lbs of seed potatoes for every 10 yard row.

Early varieties should be planted in March; maincrop var-ieties in April. In order to decide how many rows of potatoes to plant you will want to know what yield to expect: for 1 lb of seed potatoes of a good cropping variety, you should harvest 20 lbs of potatoes.

Buy the seed potatoes in February. If you have a

greenhouse or a shed with good big windows, or a room in your house which is not in use, put them out into shallow trays or boxes or on newspaper on the floor, placing them so that the end with most 'eyes' is upward. The eyes will produce short, stout sprouts so that your seed potatoes will be growing even before you plant them.

Trenches for planting should be 6 inches deep—I am assuming the soil has been dug and manured with compost as described in Chapter 3. If you happen to have any grass mowings, dead leaves, or withered weeds, or straw, put some into the trenches. Put the seed potatoes, sprouts upwards, into the trenches which should be 20 inches apart, at 12 inch intervals. Refill the trenches, firm the soil, and rake it lightly.

Foliage will appear above the ground surprisingly quickly. As there is still some danger of frost in April, and as potatoes are tender, rake soil over it to cover it again—not deeply, of course, less than an inch of soil will give protection. The foliage will soon push through again. When it is about 6 inches high, rake the soil from both sides of the row up to it but this time don't cover it, leave the foliage above the soil. The idea is to make ridges so that young potatoes growing near the surface are well covered. This earthing-up should be repeated from time to time as the potatoes grow. Keep the soil between the rows tilled with the hoe (or rotovator: see Appendix iv).

Harvesting is in three stages. In June you can dig new potatoes from the early crop when the 'haulms'—the foliage complex—is still green and growing. Then there is an intermediate stage when you may dig up maincrop potatoes while the haulms are still green and vigorous. But the main harvest for storing and use later, is dug up when the haulms are dying down or are quite withered.

Pests and diseases   There is only one pest and one disease the amateur grower need know anything about. And neither is very likely to occur. The pest is the Colorado Beetle: the disease is Potato Blight, a fungus disease. The magnificent work of the Ministry of Agriculture has kept the beetle out of Britain, but from time to time there is an invasion from the Continent and it is the duty of any citizen who finds one on his potato plants to report it to the police.   The beetles are twice the size of a ladybird, bright yellow, striped and spotted with black.   The grubs are orange in colour.   Potato Blight, which caused the terrible Irish famine in 1846, is a fungus disease.   It is no longer of pandemic proportions or even very common but where there is any danger of it, *eg* in persistently warm, wet summers, it can be prevented from spreading by spraying the potato foliage with a copper based fungicide.   The organism which causes this disease is called *Phytophthora infestans*, as well it may be.   It is first noticed as dark brown patches on the edges of the leaves.   Turn the leaves over and under the patches you will find matching patches of whitey-grey mould.   If you do not at once use a fungicide and if the weather is warm but wet, this quickly spreads, the leaves and stems turn black as if burnt, and they stink.   Long before this stage, the fungus spores have been washed into the ground and are growing on the actual potatoes, which begin to rot.

Radish   A continuous supply of radishes from May till the end of October can be obtained by a succession of sowings of seed from mid-March to mid-September.   As you will not need very large quantities all at one time, sow short rows of radishes once every three weeks during that period in some part of the garden which would otherwise not be in use—for example, between the celery rows, between the runner bean rows or the rows of peas.   They will not be there long enough to get in the way unless you're using a rotovator, in which case 'catch cropping' between rows is not possible.

A deep, fine tilth gives the best results.   Sow the seed in drills an inch deep, cover and make firm.   Rows need not be more than 6 inches apart.   You should either take the trouble to space the seeds an inch apart when sowing; or face the fact that the seedlings will have to be thinned to an inch apart as soon as they are large enough to handle.

Spring and early summer radishes require no care except weeding by hand or hoe.   Mid-summer radishes usually require some watering.

Shallots   These useful onions can be, but are not, grown from seed but from bulbs.   A single shallot bulb planted in the soil produces a number of offset bulbs as it grows, giving a six or seven-fold increase. You buy the bulbs from late October onwards in garden shops.

Having prepared a tilth, plant the bulbs by pressing them into the soil, along a straight line to about half their depth, so that the pointed end remains well above the soil surface. Put them 6 inches apart. If your garden is hand hoed, rows need not be more than 12 inches apart; if a rotovator is used, then the rows should be 20 inches apart.

Planting is best done in mid-December but can be done as late as February. The shallots should be harvested in July. Lift all the bulbs, clean them of soil, leave them on any dry ground in the sun till the leaves are withered and store in a cool, dry place.

Spinach must be grown on deep, moist, well-tilled soil and watered whenever the weather is dry. As it takes only a few weeks from seed to harvest, it saves space to grow it between the rows of slower-growing crops, because it will soon be over and out of the way. But you cannot do this if a rotovator is used. If it is not grown between other crops—peas or beans for instance—but by itself, the rows should be 12 inches apart. Sow the seed in drills 1 inch deep in fine tilth, cover and firm. Keep down weeds by hoeing. The first sowing can be done in March and if you like spinach, once a fortnight thereafter until August.

Spinach for winter use should be sown in mid-September with another sowing a fortnight later. It will stand the cold of an average winter but is spoilt by severe cold or really persistent rain and snow.

Summer spinach must be harvested as soon as it is ready, for it quickly runs to seed if left too long and becomes useless.

Spinach beet is a variety of beetroot only instead of eating the root you eat the leaves which are a substitute for spinach. In my opinion it is an inferior vegetable but many would not agree. For cultivation see *Beetroot*.

Swede For cultivation, see *Turnip*. Swede seeds are sown in May or June.

Sweet corn is a variety of maize, used as a vegetable (Corn on the Cob). It is grown from seed which should not be sown in the open before the last week in May. Alternatively you can sow the seed, one to a small pot, in pots under glass in mid April, and plant the seedlings out in late May after hardening off. Drills for sowing should be 2 inches deep and seed sown one every six inches to be on the safe side. The seedlings are thinned so that the interval between them is 12 inches when they are about 6 inches tall, by pulling out every other plant if all the seeds germinate. Usually, they don't: you get several seedlings 6 inches apart, then gaps where several have failed. So use the seedlings you remove from the over-crowded parts of the row to fill in the gaps.

Harvest the cobs when the corn grains are fully formed—the size of a large pea—but still milky white or pale yellow.

Turnip If you want turnips all the year round, or at least for as long as possible, the first sowing of seed should be made in the second half of March, successional sowings made at 3 week intervals thereafter until the end of June, and the maincrop sowing for winter use late in August. The turnips from all the early sowings should be used when they are small. Treat them as a 'catch crop', quickly making way for more important vegetables.

Sow thinly in 1 inch deep drills on well-dug, finely tilled, moist soil. If there is any choice, turnips do better on light than on heavy soil. Rows should be 20 inches apart. (It can be less, but 20 inches is necessary where a rotovator is used). Sow the seed by dropping a very small pinch of it into the drills at 6 inch intervals. Fill in with soil and make it firm. When the seedlings come up, thin each group to one. Alternatively, you can sow the seed thinly all along the drill, thin the seedlings to 3 inches apart, and then thin again to 6 inches, using the thinnings, very small turnips, for cooking.

Turnip 'tops'—leaves, can be used as if they were spinach but you cannot cut off all the leaves and still expect to get useable roots, so the roots must be allowed to attain a useful size before leaves are cut for cooking.

A good variety for the first sowing is Early Winter Milan,

and for the winter keeping crop, Manchester Market.

Pests and diseases If the soil in which turnips and swedes are grown is not adequately limed, they may suffer, like cabbages, from the Club Root disease; so a dressing of lime is the best preventative. No other disease or pest is likely to be troublesome where cultivation is clean and composting is practised as a routine.

NOTE Use of manure and fertilizer: refer back to pp.27-29.

THE HERB GARDEN

Culinary herbs can be grown wherever you have room for them. In the plans that follow it might be a good idea to grow them in one long row, or two if you need so many herbs, between rows of fruit trees. On the other hand it is pleasant to grow them in a small, ornamental herb-garden near the kitchen door if the conditions in which you are gardening make that possible. With that in mind I have included here three suggested designs, but many gardeners will prefer to draw their own original designs.

I will put these culinary herbs into the same 'dictionary' form as the vegetables. The herbs everyone needs are in bold type; those which only enthusiasts will want to grow, in italics.

Angelica Foliage is used to make an infusion and stems for candying. A few pieces of stem cooked or bottled with rhubarb reduces tartness. Sow the seeds in a drill in the nursery bed in late August or September. If you sow thinly enough, or thin thoroughly, you can leave the seedlings there until they are ready to plant out in November. The plants will reach their usable size in the following year but fresh seed must then be sown as the plants die at the end of their second season.

Basil Sow seed under glass in April. Prick out as soon as seedlings are large enough to handle. Harden off in early May and plant out in late May. When the plants come into flower cut them off at ground level, tie in bunches, and hang in a shady place to dry for winter use. If you like Basil fresh rather than dried, grow a few plants in pots,

55

pinch out the flower buds and move the pots into the greenhouse or onto the window sill of the kitchen, in October. Basil is not hardy.

Bay leaves The leaves of the tree *Laurus nobilis*, the true laurel. The tree is more or less hardy in most of Britain though it may be cut to the ground in very severe winters. You can either buy a young tree or beg a sucker from someone else's garden. Bay laurel will grow in any soil, prefers a sunny site and is extremely vigorous. Try to keep the tree on one trunk, for if suckers are allowed to grow you get a large and unmanageable clump. The leaves can be used fresh, or you can cut and hang small branches to dry the leaves and store them in a dry jar.

Chervil Sow the seed outside from late February in small sowings at monthly intervals until October. This gives you

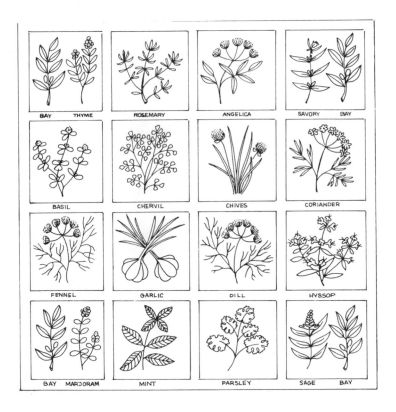

BAY THYME	ROSEMARY	ANGELICA	SAVORY BAY
BASIL	CHERVIL	CHIVES	CORIANDER
FENNEL	GARLIC	DILL	HYSSOP
BAY MARJORAM	MINT	PARSLEY	SAGE BAY

a constant supply, for cutting the leaves throughout spring, summer and autumn. It should be used like parsley.

Chives Sow the seeds outside in April, preferably on their permanent site, and thin them out so that they grow in small clusters about 6 inches apart. Cut the leaves as required and prevent flowering if you can by removing flower buds (though the flowers are pretty). Your row or bed of chives will yield well for four or five years, but it is then best to raise a new lot from seed. You can, however, increase your stock by lifting a cluster, dividing it into smaller clusters and replanting them 6 inches apart.

Coriander An ingredient of curry powders and often used in Spanish cuisine. Sow the seed outside in April, thin the seedlings to three or four inches apart, keep weeded and watered and wait until the seeds ripen in August. Cut and

57

c

Bunch the plants and hang the bunches in a shady place to dry. Thresh the seeds by beating the heads of the bunches on clean sheets of newspaper, and store for use in a clean, dry jar.

Dill Sow in drill in April. Thin the seedlings to 6 inches apart. Keep hoed, weeded and watered as necessary. Most people use only the fresh leaves as needed, but the seeds can be ripened, threshed and stored like Coriander (above), for winter use.

Fennel Sow the seeds in drills outside in April and thin to 10 inches apart. Fennel is a tall and elegant perennial and if the leaves are used moderately, as needed, the plants will last for years. But flowering stalks should be cut out as soon as identified to encourage more leaf growth.

Garlic A bulb of the onion family. Buy three or four good garlic bulbs in February and break them up into their component 'cloves' which separate very easily. Plant in a fine tilth of soil rich in compost, by dibbing small holes 9 inches apart and dropping a clove into each hole. The cloves should be only just covered, the pointed end being just below the soil. Keep clear of weeds and well-watered. Lift and store the crop in autumn when the foliage has withered. You can replant at once, using your own garlic cloves, if you do not want to wait until February.

Hyssop A small shrub with either blue, pink or white flowers. Sow seeds in April, prick out when the seedlings can be handled and plant out to 12 inches apart. Can be used as an edging plant. Cut back from time to time to maintain bushiness.

Marjoram, also called **Origanum** The kind to grow in Britain is Pot Marjoram. Sow the seeds in April, prick out as soon as they are manageable, and plant into their permanent sites, 8 inches apart, in late May. It is a small sub-shrub and plants will last for years. Increase stock as required from cuttings taken in July and rooted in small pots under glass.

Mint There are four species in common use and innumerable varieties, some of them ornamental. The one most commonly grown is Spearmint, but the round-leaved mint, Pennyroyal, is superior in flavour. No point in growing mint from seed. Beg a piece of the underground stem with one or more 'nodes' on it, in March, plant in a shallow trench in moist soil, and you will very soon have more mint than you know what to do with. The chief problem in cultivating mint is to prevent it from taking over the whole garden.

Origanum See *Marjoram*

Parsley As parsley is a biennial and as it is the one herb of which a continuous supply is required, sow a first lot in February, a second in early May and a third in July—for winter use, all out of doors. The winter crop should, if possible, be given a warm site, *eg* at the foot of a south wall. Sow thinly in shallow drills 12 inches apart. Seed takes from five to six weeks to germinate. Thin seedlings to 3 inches apart. Parsely does best in richly manured soil. The winter crop may need protecting with cloches. The useful life of the plants can be prolonged by cutting out flowering stems as soon as they can be identified by their thick, coarse habit.

Rosemary One or two bushes of this shrub should suffice, so it can be bought from a nursery rather than raised from seed. There is a white-flowered as well as the common blue-flowered, rosemary; and a very pretty form with gold variegated leaves. All are equally useful in cooking. The bushes need a sunny site and if protection from the north-east is possible, so much the better. They will grow in any soil, but a gravelly rather than a dry one is best. Easily increased by cuttings taken in July. The only care required, apart from keeping the bushes clear of weeds, is pinching-out the topmost growing tips from time to time in order to maintain bushiness. Rosemary is not absolutely hardy in our climate and may be injured by cold in severe winters.

Rue is far too bitter to be used in cooking for modern tastes, but a herb garden seems incomplete without it. You can but should not raise it from seed, because the most attractive variety, Jackman's Blue, does not come true from seed. So buy a plant of that variety and increase stocks by taking cuttings in July and rooting them under glass. Rue will grow in any soil and excepting for occasional pinching-out or cutting back to prevent it becoming too leggy, requires no care but keeping clear of weeds. *Warning*. A few people are allergic to rue. Although rare the allergy causes a severe skin eruption.

Sage Sow the seeds in 1 inch drills, outside in April. Prick out as soon as seedlings can be handled. Plant into their permanent sites in June or July, 12 inches apart. Sage is a shrub and the plants will last for years but will grow very leggy unless the topmost growing tips are pinched out from time to time. Will grow in any soil and requires only to be kept clear of weeds.

Savory Summer savory: sow the seeds in early April in 1 inch drills 12 inches apart and thin the seedlings to 6 inches apart. When you cut a plant off for use, the stump will sprout again, but this is an annual species and must be sown again in the following April. On the other hand, Winter Savory is a hardy, semi-evergreen perennial.   Raise in the same way as Summer Savory.   Both can be cut and dried for winter use.

Tea   I do not seriously suggest that you grow your own tea, but as this book is about subsistence gardening it is fair to point out that if you can find out how to process the leaves, there's no particular difficulty in growing the plant in the west, south-west, and south of Britain, on acid soils (*p*H below 7).   The plant is *Camellia sinensis* and is not as ruggedly hardy as the ornamental camellia (*C. japonica*) varieties.   It is a woody shrub from 3 to 6 feet tall, and requires a lot of water, peaty soil, and warm summers.   Messrs Hillier of Winchester list the plant in their great catalogue.

Thyme   Our native, prostrate thyme has the same scent as the culinary herb which, however, is a bushy sub-shrub.   Sow seeds in April, prick out, and plant into the permanent sites 12 inches apart.   The plants, kept bushy by picking out the top-most shoots when fresh Thyme is wanted in the kitchen, will last for years.   They are best on light soil in full sun, require very little compost feeding, and should be kept clear of weeds.

CHAPTER 5   THE ANNUAL CYCLE IN THE 300
SQUARE YARD PLOT

Please look at the diagram on page 63.   It represents a plot which is 30 yards x 10 yards and is the shape of many thousands of allotment gardens and suburban back gardens.   Of course there is a small area occupied by compost bins, a toolshed, cold frames and a nursery bed.

An objection will spring at once to the minds of many readers: 'My garden isn't that shape.   It's smaller . . . larger . . . shorter . . . wider . . . no shape at all . . . triangular . . .'   I know: but the point of working from this very common 300 square yard unit is that it is a unit of known size and regular shape and as such can be used as a yard-stick by which to measure the work to be done and the amount of crops to be planted and expected.   The outlines on p. 64 are not merely an exercise in geometry: drawn to a scale of 0.05 inch to the yard (1:720), each one contains 300 square yards of surface.   I believe that makes the only point needed in this case; and we can work with the 30 x 10 shape without further apologies.   Used in conjunction with the vegetable dictionary on pp. 38-55 and the working-time and yield information on pp. 80-86, it is applicable to a food garden of any shape or any size.

The principal purpose of the following pages is to explain the means by which a continuous supply of vegetable crops is maintained, waxing in mid summer and waning in mid winter but never failing.   The monthly tables of the cycle start on p. 67.

I have begun by supposing what is almost impossible, a garden—our 10 x 30 yard unit plot—completely full on November 1st.   This could only happen if you planted solely for winter crops and took nothing from the garden in the summer.   But one has to start somewhere: the plant-harvest

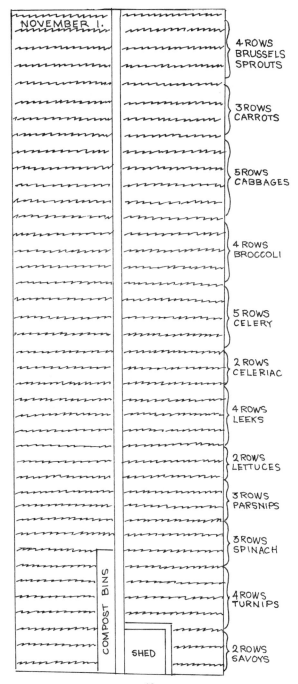

NOVEMBER 1.

4 ROWS
BRUSSELS
SPROUTS

3 ROWS
CARROTS

5 ROWS
CABBAGES

4 ROWS
BROCCOLI

5 ROWS
CELERY

2 ROWS
CELERIAC

4 ROWS
LEEKS

2 ROWS
LETTUCES

3 ROWS
PARSNIPS

3 ROWS
SPINACH

4 ROWS
TURNIPS

2 ROWS
SAVOYS

COMPOST BINS

SHED

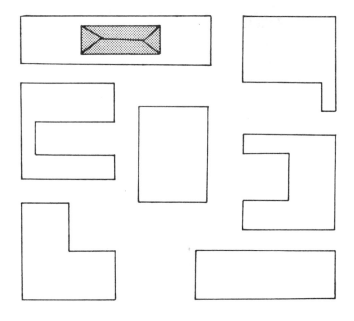

Scale: 0.05 in. = 1 yd.

cycle is eternal and one has to break into it at some point.   As
you will see, the November 1 at the end of the cycle does not
work out quite the same, though by the time your broad beans
are sown in November, there will be about a half row of fallow.

The reason why one cannot simply cram the garden with
summer crops is forward-planning: certain winter crops take
many months to grow and must occupy land without yielding
an immediate or even swift harvest—brussels sprouts, celery,
parsnips are examples.

A number of points about this cycle plan need explana-
tion.   On the plan it looks as if whole rows of crops are harvested at one fell swoop.   In practice, of course, this is not
so.   The crops of that row will be used from day to day and
may take a whole month to clear.   But short of presenting the
plan as an animated cartoon, or making it 365 pages long, only
completed states can be shown—full rows or empty ones.   The
point is that a row is either occupied by a particular crop or is
not.   If it is, it makes no difference how much of that crop is
left *in situ* on any given day.

In this kind of intensive horticulture which we are practising, we do not wait for a row to be entirely cleared of one crop before starting to plant its successor. You can and should fill up the row with the successor crop as fast as you clear part of it of the first. As carrots or turnips are pulled you can move in cabbage or broccoli plants from the nursery. And so on: a continuous smooth process; not a series of lurches.

Of course, to practise this craft you need a continuous supply of young plants, in other words a nursery-bed. This is provided for in the plan and if the nursery work suggested in column 2 of the monthly tables is carried out, sowing small amounts of seed each time and thinning out the seedlings as soon as they are big enough to handle, you will have a continuous supply of nursery stock for planting into the garden as required.

This cyclic plan is designed to be used in conjunction with the Vegetable Dictionary on pp. 38-55. For example, in the plan you read 'Broad Beans: sow 4 rows' or 'Shallots: plant 4 rows'. All very well, but if you happen to be a novice—how? Turn up 'Broad Beans' or 'Shallots' or whatever in the Vegetable Dictionary, and it will tell you how.

A very important point: the plan in the following pages is *not meant to be followed literally*. If the choice and proportions of vegetables in the plan happens to match your tastes, well and good—follow it exactly. But it is intended to show how you can crop your unit plot continuously; you can, by consulting the Vegetable Dictionary, substitute another crop for one in the plan. For example, I have not included Marrows because I don't think they are worth the space; you may think otherwise. I have given a low place to beetroot; you may wish to promote it and, as the football journalists say, 'relegate' lettuce or turnips to the second league. So use the plan as your own if you want to, as a general guide if you don't like my choice or my proportions.

May I enlarge briefly on that? On the plan, potatoes occupy a lot of space from March to October. Potatoes are cheap: you may decide to buy rather than grow, and to increase your salad or brassica crops. Again, the only summer vegetable which is as good quick-frozen as it is fresh is green peas. You might decide to leave them out of the plan and grow more brassicas or marrows or something else.

A couple of minor points: why, with 2 rows of celeriac in the garden when we first took it over, did I eliminate it in the following season? Because to accommodate summer and autumn crops, a crop needing many months to mature had to be left out and celeriac, is to my mind, by no means a staple. Why no cauliflowers? If you will look at the Vegetable Dictionary you will see that there is no difference between cauliflower and broccoli: I use the word broccoli to mean both. Spinach in the plan can also mean spinach-beet which is hardier in winter.

The word 'harvest' here means harvesting either to eat at once, or to store. You may store in a deep freezer, but please see the Appendix about this treatment. Or you may store by conventional methods. Onions, once dried, can be stored by hanging in bunches in a dry shed. Carrots are best stored by stowing them in deep boxes or heaps between layers of sand. A really big crop of turnips or potatoes is best stored in a clamp. You do it like this: first, lay down a bed of clean, dry straw about a foot deep. Onto it heap your potatoes or turnips, dry and reasonably clean, in the form of a pyramid, or a ridge. Now cover them with a thatch of more clean, dry straw, about a foot thick, combing it with your fingers so that it is vertical, up-and-down. This is important because the individual straws thus form a system of tubes to carry rainwater down to the soil, keeping it off your potatoes or turnips. Next, make two or three beer-bottle size bundles of straws, and so place them round the top of the pyramid or along the ridge that they stand up like chimneys. Leave them sticking out when—the next stage—you cover the whole with earth about 6 inches deep. The straw chimneys ventilate the clamp without letting rain in.

Don't forget that the plans on the following pages tell you *when* to do what you have to do, but not *how*. For *how* you must refer to Chapter 4, The Vegetable Dictionary.

One other thing: you'll notice that, in the plans, I have given a separate place to Savoys. Savoys are just one kind of cabbage; but they are more ruggedly hardy than any other and will survive the severest winters. So they deserve being treated as a special vegetable. Substitute something else if you feel that this idea is a lot of nonsense.

START CYCLE

Start cycle	Nursery work	Plant	Harvest	State at 1 November
Brussels Sprouts				4 rows
Cabbage				5 rows
Carrots				3 rows
Brocolli				4 rows
Celery				4 rows
Celeriac				2 rows
Leeks				4 rows
Lettuce				2 rows
Parsnips				3 rows
Spinach				3 rows
Turnips				4 rows
Savoys				2 rows
Broad beans				
Shallots				
Peas				
Onions				
Potatoes				
Radish				
French beans				
Runner beans				
Fallow				
				40 rows

N.B. Dates are based on S. England. In the North they may be two weeks later.

NOVEMBER

November	Nursery work	Plant	Harvest	State at 1 December
Brussels Sprouts			2 rows	2 rows
Cabbage				5 rows
Carrots			1 row	2 rows
Brocolli			1 row	3 rows
Celery			1 row	3 rows
Celeriac				2 rows
Leeks				4 rows
Lettuce			1 row	1 row
Parsnips				3 rows
Spinach			1 row	2 rows
Turnips			1 row	3 rows
Savoys				2 rows
Broad beans		Sow 4 rows		4 rows
Shallots				
Peas				
Onions				
Potatoes				
Radish				
French beans				
Runner beans				
Fallow				4 rows
				40 rows

DECEMBER

December	Nursery work	Plant	Harvest	State at 1 January
Brussels Sprouts			1 row	1 row
Cabbage			1 row	4 rows
Carrots			1 row	1 row
Brocolli				3 rows
Celery			1 row	2 rows
Celeriac				2 rows
Leeks			1 row	3 rows
Lettuce			1 row	
Parsnips				3 rows
Spinach			1 row	1 row
Turnips			1 row	2 rows
Savoys				2 rows
Broad beans				4 rows
Shallots		Plant 4 rows		4 rows
Peas				
Onions				
Potatoes				
Radish				
French beans				
Runner beans				
Fallow				8 rows
				40 rows

JANUARY

January	Nursery work	Plant	Harvest	State at 1 February
Brussels Sprouts			1 row	
Cabbage	Sow under glass			4 rows
Carrots			½ row	½ row
Brocolli	Sow under glass		½ row	2½ rows
Celery			1 row	1 row
Celeriac				2 rows
Leeks			½ row	2½ rows
Lettuce				
Parsnips			1 row	2 rows
Spinach			1 row	
Turnips			1 row	1 row
Savoys				2 rows
Broad beans				4 rows
Shallots				4 rows
Peas				
Onions				
Potatoes				
Radish				
French beans				
Runner beans				
Fallow				14½ rows
				40 rows

70

FEBRUARY

February	Nursery work	Plant	Harvest	State at 1 March
Brussels Sprouts	Sow under glass			
Cabbage	Sow under glass		1 row	3 rows
Carrots			½ row	
Brocolli	Sow under glass		½ row	2 rows
Celery			1 row	
Celeriac			½ row	1½ rows
Leeks	Sow under glass		1 row	1½ rows
Lettuce	Sow under glass			
Parsnips			1 row	1 row
Spinach				
Turnips			½ row	½ row
Savoys			1 row	1 row
Broad beans		Sow 1 row		5 rows
Shallots				4 rows
Peas		Sow 1 row		1 row
Onions				
Potatoes				
Radish				
French beans				
Runner beans				
Fallow				19½ rows
				40 rows

MARCH

March	Nursery work	Plant	Harvest	State at 1 April
Brussels Sprouts				
Cabbage			1 row	2 rows
Carrots		Sow 2 rows		2 rows
Brocolli	Sow open nursery		½ row	1½ rows
Celery	Sow under glass			
Celeriac	Sow under glass		1 row	½ row
Leeks			1½ rows	
Lettuce	Sow under glass	Sow 1 row		1 row
Parsnips		Sow 3 rows	1 row	3 rows
Spinach		Sow 1 row		1 row
Turnips		Sow 1 row	½ row	1 row
Savoys			1 row	
Broad beans				5 rows
Shallots				4 rows
Peas		Sow 2 rows		3 rows
Onions		Sow 3 rows		3 rows
Potatoes		Plant 3 rows		3 rows
Radish		Sow as catch crop		
French beans	Sow under glass			
Runner beans				
Fallow				10 rows
				40 rows

APRIL

April	Nursery work	Plant	Harvest	State at 1 May
Brussels Sprouts				
Cabbage	Sow open nursery		1 row	1 row
Carrots		Sow 1 row		3 rows
Brocolli	Sow open nursery		1½ rows	
Celery				
Celeriac			½ row	
Leeks	Sow open nursery			
Lettuce		Plant 1 row		2 rows
Parsnips				3 rows
Spinach		Sow 1 row		2 rows
Turnips		Sow as catch crop	½ row	½ row
Savoys	Sow open nursery			
Broad beans				5 rows
Shallots				4 rows
Peas		Sow 1 row		4 rows
Onions		Plant 3 rows of sets		6 rows
Potatoes		Plant 4 rows		7 rows
Radish		Sow as catch crop		
French beans				
Runner beans	Sow under glass			
Fallow				2½ rows
				40 rows

May	Nursery work	Plant	Harvest	State at 1 June
Brussels Sprouts		Plant 1 row		1 row
Cabbage	Sow open nursery	Plant 1 row	1 row	1 row
Carrots				3 rows
Brocolli	Sow open nursery	Plant 1 row		1 row
Celery				
Celeriac				
Leeks				
Lettuce		Plant 1 row	1 row	2 rows
Parsnips				3 rows
Spinach			1 row	1 row
Turnips			½ row	
Savoys				
Broad beans			1 row	4 rows
Shallots				4 rows
Peas		Sow 1 row	1 row	4 rows
Onions				6 rows
Potatoes				7 rows
Radish		Sow as catch crop	Some	
French beans		Plant 1 row		1 row
Runner beans		Plant 1 row		1 row
Fallow				1 row
				40 rows

JUNE

June	Nursery work	Plant	Harvest	State at 1 July
Brussels Sprouts		Plant 3 rows		4 rows
Cabbage		Plant 1 row		2 rows
Carrots			1 row	2 rows
Brocolli		Plant 2 rows		3 rows
Celery		Plant 2 rows		2 rows
Celeriac				
Leeks		Plant 2 rows		2 rows
Lettuce	Sow open nursery	Plant 1 row	1 row	2 rows
Parsnips				3 rows
Spinach			1 row	
Turnips		Sow ½ row		½ row
Savoys				
Broad beans			2 rows	2 rows
Shallots			4 rows	
Peas			1 row	3 rows
Onions			1 row	5 rows
Potatoes			2 rows	5 rows
Radish		Sow as catch crop	Some	
French beans		Sow 1 row		2 rows
Runner beans				1 row
Beetroot		Sow 1 row		1 row
Fallow				½ row
				40 rows

75

JULY

July	Nursery work	Plant	Harvest	State at 1 August
Brussels Sprouts				4 rows
Cabbage		Plant 2 rows		4 rows
Carrots		Sow 3 rows	1 row	4 rows
Brocolli		Plant 1 row		4 rows
Celery		Plant 1 row		3 rows
Celeriac				
Leeks		Plant 2 rows		4 rows
Lettuce			1 row	1 row
Parsnips				3 rows
Spinach				
Turnips		Sow ½ row	½ row	½ row
Savoys		Plant 1 row		1 row
Broad beans			2 rows	
Shallots				
Peas			3 rows	
Onions			1 row	4 rows
Potatoes			1 row	4 rows
Radish		Sow as catch crop	Some	
French beans			1 row	1 row
Runner beans				1 row
Beetroot				1 row
Fallow				½ row
				40 rows

AUGUST

August	Nursery work	Plant	Harvest	State at 1 September
Brussels Sprouts				4 rows
Cabbage		Plant 1 row	1 row	4 rows
Carrots		Sow 1 row	1 row	4 rows
Brocolli		Plant 1 row	1 row	4 rows
Celery				3 rows
Celeriac				
Leeks				4 rows
Lettuce		Plant 1 row	1 row	1 row
Parsnips				3 rows
Spinach		Sow 1 row		1 row
Turnips		Sow 2 rows	½ row	2 rows
Savoys		Plant 1 row		2 rows
Broad beans				
Shallots				
Peas				
Onions			1 row	3 rows
Potatoes			1 row	3 rows
Radish		Sow as catch crop	Some	
French beans			1 row	
Runner beans		Harvest some but row remains		1 row
Beetroot				1 row
				40 rows

77

 # SEPTEMBER

September	Nursery work	Plant	Harvest	State at 1 October
Brussels Sprouts				4 rows
Cabbage		Plant 3 rows	1 row	6 rows
Carrots			½ row	3½ rows
Brocolli		Plant 1 row	1 row	4 rows
Celery				3 rows
Celeriac				
Leeks				4 rows
Lettuce		Plant 1 row	1 row	1 row
Parsnips				3 rows
Spinach		Sow 1 row		2 rows
Turnips		Sow 2 rows		4 rows
Savoys				2 rows
Broad beans				
Shallots				
Peas				
Onions			3 rows	
Potatoes			3 rows	
Radish		Sow as catch crop	Some	
French beans				
Runner beans		Harvest but row remains		1 row
Beetroot				1 row
Fallow				1½ rows
				40 rows

OCTOBER

October	Nursery work	Plant	Harvest	State at 1 November
Brussels Sprouts				4 rows
Cabbage			1 row	5 rows
Carrots			½ row	3 rows
Brocolli			1 row	4 rows
Celery				3 rows
Leeks				4 rows
Lettuce		Plant 1 row	1 row	1 row
Parsnips				3 rows
Spinach			½ row	1½ rows
Turnips			½ row	3½ rows
Savoys				2 rows
Broad beans				
Shallots				
Peas				
Onions				
Potatoes				
Radish			Some	
French beans				
Runner beans			Finish harvest	
Beetroot			1 row	
Fallow				7 rows
				40 rows

How much time will it cost you?

The question is not an easy one to answer for the manifest reason that we are not all equally strong and energetic and vary widely in speed of working. However, I shall do my best. Please refer to p. 68 of the annual cycle plan on the 300 square yard plot.

November

There are three jobs to be done in November: harvesting crops as required in the kitchen, a matter of a few minutes every day and not worth counting; the sowing of 4 rows of Broad Beans: an hour should be enough; and the hoeing of the whole area which, in a garden of this size, will be done by hand.

In an average November it is probable that weeds will still be growing although not, of course, as vigorously as earlier in the year. You might get away with a single hoeing in the month, but we should reckon on two. Although an experienced man can hoe a 10 yard row, (including the space between the rows), in 15 minutes, working at the steady pace proper to gardening and doing the job thoroughly, we will allow half an hour for each row.

In the month of November, then: 21 hours. By November it will be too dark to work in the garden much after 4 o'clock which means that for the man or woman in ordinary employment, we are left with only the four weekends: so, 5 hours out of each weekend must be given to the garden. In practice you will soon get it down to 4 hours—say every Saturday morning, or Sunday morning.

December

Only one essential job; planting the shallots. An hour will be ample. But what about hoeing? In the years 1972, 1973 and 1974 weeds were still growing strongly (so was everything else excepting deciduous trees and shrubs). In many years, however, the garden is more or less dormant in December. And another point: it may well be impossible to 'get on the land', for the soil may be too wet to work on. You cannot hoe water-logged soil and even if you could, you should not do so.

I suggest that with luck you should be able to get on the land two weekends out of the four. Give that 10 hours to digging, (if you are a digger), to barrowing compost from the bins to rows which have been entirely cleared, spreading it and, if the soil be workable, lightly forking it into the top three or four inches. I doubt whether you will need to give the garden more than 12 hours in December.

Total to date—33 hours

January

As a general rule there is nothing which has to be done in a vegetable garden in January but providing you can get on the land, that is to say the weather has been dry but not freezing, you can spend a few hours barrowing and spreading compost, digging (if you're a digger), and forking over the composted land, as rows are cleared. In January, then, 10 hours at most.

Total to date: 43 hours

February

Again, it's a question of weather permitting: it may be too wet to work in the garden, or the ground may be frozen hard. An hour is enough for that row of broad beans and the first row of peas. For the rest, digging, compost-spreading and forking-over of cleared rows should not take you more than 12 hours in the month, supposing garden work to be possible.

Total to date: 55 hours

March

Lighter evenings; you may be able to get a few hours in during the week, as well as weekends. Assuming the work of digging, or composting-and-forking, cleared rows to be complete, you had better allow 10 hours for planting and sowing. And another 10 hours for preparing the rows cleared during the month, for their next crop. Twenty hours is the minimum the garden will demand in March.

Total to date: 75 hours

April

The situation should be more or less the same as March. Sowing and planting, allow 10 hours. There should now be a little less compost-barrowing, forking over, and digging. On the other hand, hoeing now starts in earnest. Your garden will probably demand about 25 hours of your time in April.

Total to date: 100 hours

May

A busy month but at least you now have long, light evenings. Planting out young brassica plants takes longer than sowing seeds. Allow 15 hours, though you may do it in less time as you get into the swing of it. You will have to hoe over at least 32 rows which will take you 16 hours if you do it thoroughly. It looks like 31 hours but you will be beginning to remake compost heaps and clear the second, and if you have one, third bin. Preparing the runner-bean supports will take a couple of hours. Better allow 35 hours—but that's only an hour per evening and a little extra at weekends: or, if you want your weekends free, an hour and a half each evening—pleasant, healthy exercise.

Total to date: 135 hours

June

Even busier. You can get through the planting job in 15 hours but hoeing frequency rises as weeds are at their most vigorous, you will have to do some irrigation, though if you use the recommended method that will not take much time. Don't try hoeing recently irrigated rows: hoe first, irrigate afterwards. A lot of jobs take very little time—five minutes to scatter the fertiliser on a ten-yard row. Call it 35 hours.

Total to date: 170 hours

July

Much the same. You will have cleared rows to compost and fork over, celery to earth up, at least 30 rows to hoe twice, and planting out will take between 10 and 12 hours. This, and all the months since March, will demand an hour or two at the nursery bed and cold frames. Still, 35 hours is enough.

Total to date: 205 hours

August

Take a look at the Plans for July and August. There isn't much in it. We'll allow 35 hours again.

Total to date: 240 hours

September

I am going to assume that in August you took a holiday and that for 2 or 3 weeks the garden was neglected. So now you have to catch up: weeds have grown alarmingly; rows which should have been dug or composted and forked over, have been left unworked. So that as well as the routine work necessary in this month, which will demand about 30 hours, you will have a lot to do to restore order. You may have to allow 6 hours of each of your 4 weekends and almost an hour every evening of the working days, say a total for the month of 40 hours.

Total to date: 280 hours

October

You'll still be hoeing and there'll be more digging, compost-spreading and forking in to be done; but hardly any time required for planting. 25 hours should cover it.

Total for the year: 305 hours

Three hundred and five hours: the sceptical reader will ask—what is your timing criterion? It has been arrived at by compromising between the time which I take to do the work and the time taken by my gardener, an old age pensioner whom I employ for 2 hours a day, 4 days a week so that I can give my own time to the trees, shrubs and perennials of the other part of the garden. I am an impatient and therefore fast worker; Alf is a hale seventy-eight; he has, therefore, more than half a century of experience, but is a shade slower than a younger man would be.

What do you get for your time?

The answer to this question is so imprecise that one tries to avoid answering it. I shall make an attempt because the reader has a right to an answer of some kind. For the purpose of doing so I have to make certain assumptions; if your results fall short of my estimate, do please bear them in mind before abusing me. They are, one, that you have followed the plan fairly closely; and two, that you have suffered no more than a reasonable percentage of failures and set-backs. For the rest, my estimates are conservative. Now turn to the table on p. 86.

The real value

To that £230 worth of food we have to add something: young carrots, turnips, and lettuce—the thinnings—have not been counted. There are the benefits which cannot be quantified in terms of money—freshness, vitamin bonus, freedom from the burden of shopping for vegetables. Call the annual money value of your crop £250. Set it against the normal expenditure of a four-person household on fresh and frozen vegetables. What it comes to is this, put as starkly as I can put it: given the increasing difficulty of making ends meet, the man or woman who does not particularly want to cultivate a vegetable garden, (the ones who enjoy it are another matter), is 'moonlighting'—taking an extra job on. So the question is: is that a good one to take on?

The answer is very far from simple: given that you get £250 of money's worth from your 10 rod garden, (and you will have to be good at it to do so), what does it cost you?

I am going to give two answers: one, the ordinary sensible person's answer; the other an accountant's answer.

The commonsense answer

Cost of seeds, seed potatoes and onion sets   £8

Cost of amortizing a capital investment in tools—
from £4 to £6 a piece and other 'plant',
totalling, say, £150 over a ten-year period   £15

Rent equivalent for your 300 square yards calculated
at £100 p.a. per acre   £6

Water used in irrigation   £5

Fertiliser and pest-control chemicals   £10

£44

So, you're apparently over £200 to the good, to offset against what your household would spend on fresh and frozen vegetables, and totally disregarding the fact that growing vegetables in your spare time may give you pleasure and maintain you in good health.

Accountant's answer

Two items have been left out of the above costs sheet. If the £150 spent on tools, hoses, a shed etc had been left on deposit at your bank, it would have earned you £15 a year. And there's another item missing: you have paid yourself nothing for your time. Now the least you could get away with would be £1 an hour. So we have two items to add to the debit side of the balance-sheet: £15 for lost interest; and £305 for labour. Total £320 a year. You're down on the deal by £55 a year—and probably, if you're not a good gardener, by more.

I have indulged myself in the pleasure of involving you in this argument for a particular reason: to demonstrate that, when it comes to food growing, the money standard we live by is ridiculous. Turn your 10 rod plot over to asparagus, strawberries or melons, and you can make it yield £1000 a year in money, and nothing (or almost nothing) in food value.

So, console yourself: in growing vegetables for your household, (and a surplus you can give away or sell), you are producing—at a wage rate below what you're worth in accountant's language—what the over-crowded world really needs—food, at some sacrifice of something which only half-starved goats could eat—bank notes.

Crop	Weight or number	Market price early 1975	Estimated market value £	Notes
Brussels sprouts	100 lbs	6p per lb	6	Plus sprout-tops as an extra.
Cabbages	480 lbs	10p each	24	Average weight 2 lbs.
Carrots	160 lbs	5p per lb	8	Basic mature crop; add to this thinnings of young carrots throughout the season
Broccoli	300 lbs	12p each	18	
Celery	100 head	15p each	15	
Leeks	200	10p per lb	5	4 leeks per lb.
Lettuce	350	8p each	28	Price average over the year.
Parsnips	150	6p per lb	4.50	Two to the lb.
Spinach	300 lbs	10p per lb	30	Guesswork here.
Turnips	200 lbs	6p per lb	12	Plus thinnings of young turnips.
Savoys	150 lbs	10p each	7.50	
Broad beans	200 lbs	10p per lb	20	
Shallots	120 lbs	5p per lb	5	
Peas	200 lbs	8p per lb	16	Very variable, more dependent than most on good soil and cultivation and on variety.
Onions	100 lbs	5p per lb	5	More if you used none till full-size in September.
Potatoes	280 lbs	3p per lb	8.50	
French beans	80 lbs	10p per lb	8	
Runner beans	80 lbs	10p per lb	8	Given a heavy-cropping variety. Could be less of the french and more of the runners.
Beet	30 lbs	8p per lb	2.50	
Approximate totals	*3580 lbs*		*£231 at early 1975 prices*	

PART 2 THE DOUBLE PLOT: 600 SQUARE YARDS

The basic allotment plot has, in Part 1, been confined to the production of the optimum quantity of food of the kind most of us consider essential: the plan leaves little room for personal choice, some substitution of one crop for another is possible, but not very much.

But as soon as we double the area of the unit plot, the case is different. The annual harvest can be not only much larger in quantity but much more diverse, including fruit as well as the more exotic vegetables. The first unit plot is still being cultivated more or less on the plan illustrated in Part 1 and the second one is where the vegetables and fruit described in the following two chapters are grown. If you want to get an overall picture of what this second plot will look like, turn to the diagrams on pp. 136-137 in Chapter 8.

CHAPTER 6   VEGETABLE DICTIONARY:

EXOTIC AND GREENHOUSE VEGETABLES

The first consideration must now be, what extra 'capital' equipment will be required so that the two plots, or a vegetable and fruit garden of comparable size—600 square yards—can be worked at the same time.

Only two important 'extras' will be required: more provision for making compost, *ie* more bins—two more at least and three if possible; and a rotovator.   In Appendix iv you will find a discussion of the types of small cultivating machines available to you.

The compost bins should, if possible, be grouped all together, which may entail some rearrangement of Plot 1.   The chief consideration is—can you get the material you need for them?   The doubling of the area under cultivation means that you will have more waste vegetation to dispose of.   Dung is not very difficult to come by in the country, but in towns it is very difficult indeed, though in some places the proliferation of riding schools has made a difference.   It is sometimes possible to persuade a local authority to let you have some lorry loads of dead leaves swept up from the roads.   At all events, I cannot help you, you will have to solve this problem for yourself.

Throughout this book I have deliberately played down the subject of pests and diseases.   There is, of course, no species of plant in the world which does not have its parasites and pathogens, and some authors of gardening books make so much of them that one gets the impression that the gardener's life is one long and desperate struggle to preserve the precarious health of his plants.   But it is not like that: twenty five years of practical experience have convinced me that, on the whole,

89

D

while it is very necessary to deal in good time with the pests and diseases which attack fruit trees and bushes, a well-cultivated and regularly manured kitchen garden remains free from disease and is not much troubled by pests. In the case of certain vegetables pathogens and parasites are sufficiently rare to be ignored by the amateur grower; others are more vulnerable and have been dealt with accordingly.

The next point to consider is what additional vegetables you can grow and how to grow them, which brings us logically to:

Artichoke, Globe, is a giant thistle whose flower buds are a delicious vegetable. It is, incidentally, an extremely ornamental plant. Being a perennial, once planted and growing well, it is there for years. You can raise plants from seeds but it is not advisable, many of the seedlings will prove poor plants. Either buy plants from a good nursery or beg some suckers from the good plants of a friendly gardener already growing them. The best plants, dwarf in habit and with plenty of flower buds, comes from France and Italy.

The young plants or suckers (cut from the parent roots in March) should be planted March or April, 20 inches apart in rows 40 inches apart. Prepare the rows in the previous autumn, exactly as for *asparagus* (see p. 92 below). Cultivation is also as for *asparagus*.

In the first year you will get one or two 'heads' per plant only, for cutting. In the second, four or five; in the third, fourth or fifth, six or seven. After that, dig up the plants and start again from good, strong suckers of the old ones.

In the sense that globe artichokes produce very little food from a great deal of space, they are a luxury vegetable. Only those who like their exquisite flavour will give them a row or two of precious space, but the inter-rows can be used for catch crops of lettuce, radish and spinach.

Pests and diseases None of importance.

Artichokes, Jerusalem were called artichokes because they are supposed to taste like globe artichokes (they don't). They have nothing to do with Jerusalem: the plant is a sunflower, introduced from Canada about 1620, probably via France or Holland; the French for sunflower is *girasol;* or *terneusen* in Holland. Either word could give the corruption 'Jerusalem.'

The part you eat is the tuberous root; and it is also the tubers you plant if you wish to grow artichokes. No special preparation is required in soil which is regularly dressed with compost and fertilizer. Plant the tubers 20 inches apart in rows 20 inches apart, in March, using a trowel or a dibber, and so that when covered there are 3 inches of soil over them. Keep the rows hoed free of weeds and the inter-rows rotovated.

Late in October or early in November the foliage begins to turn yellow. You can then start lifting the tubers for use. And go on doing so as and when required until February. The best way to winter-store the tubers is to leave them in the ground; they are ruggedly hardy.

It may be significant to diabetics that artichokes are rich in insulin.

Pests and diseases   None of significance.

WARNING   It is essential to make sure that all the tubers are dug up by the end of February. Any left in the ground will grow and be in the way of succeeding crops. They proliferate like mad and unless rigorously controlled become a serious weed of the vegetable garden.

Asparagus is not only among the most delicious of vegetables and very wholesome, nourishing food, it has one very great advantage from the point of view of the gardener who has room for it: being a perennial, once planted it is there for at least 25 years, increasing in productivity from its first to its tenth year or even longer. By the same token, however, the preparation for planting should be thorough.

You can raise the plants from seed by sowing on a nursery bed in April, thinning seedlings to 3 inch intervals as soon as they are big enough to handle, for transplantation one year later. But I do not recommend this; if you do raise asparatus from seed you will get a great deal of thin, primitive asparagus called 'sprue'. Better, therefore, to buy plants from a reliable producer. You can do this by ordering through your garden shop or centre. You should order during the autumn before the March in which you will plant the asparatus, for delivery in March.

There are two ways of growing asparagus: in a raised bed from below which the sub-soil has been excavated and replaced with farmyard manure; and in rows like any other crop. Since you are using a machine cultivator, you should grow in rows.   Preparation of these rows calls for a great deal of manure or compost and so, if you possibly can, arrange for a supply for this special purpose rather than empty your compost bins.

To ensure a really good supply of asparagus, you should plant three ten yard rows.   Dig out the top-soil as deep as the spade and twice as wide as the spade, putting it beside the trench.   The rows should be four feet apart—centre to centre.   Half-fill the trenches with manure—don't tread it down, just throw in enough to fill generously.   You will need about 12 cubic yards of manure to do this.   Now fork it into the sub-soil by digging over the bottom of each trench with a fork, turning the manure in, breaking up the soil, and mixing them together.   Next replace the top-soil.   You will now have three ridges above the level of the surrounding soil.   Leave them to settle down for at least the whole winter—no harm in using them for light catch crops like lettuce, radishes and young turnips.

For your three rows you will need 60 plants.   When the plants arrive in March, unpack them very carefully.   Each consists of a mass of thick, brittle, white roots from a 'crown'—the crown being one or more pointed white buds.   Using a trowel, dig out, for each plant, a hole in the ridge, deep enough to take the roots which you can spread a little, gently, with your fingers, and so that the tip bud of the crown is at least an inch and preferably two inches below the surface of the top of the ridge.   Cover completely and firm the soil with light pressure of the hands on both sides.   Plant at 18 inch intervals.

Cultivation consists in hand-weeding the ridges and *shallow* rotovation between them.   The asparagus rows will receive, on and between the ridges, the routine dressings of compost-fertilizer (see part 1, pp.27-29).   You can use the space between the ridges for catch crops of lettuce, radish, young turnips or spinach.

At the end of the growing season, probably in November, the asparagus 'fern' will turn yellow.   Cut it off level with the ridge-tops and put the cuttings on the compost heap.   Do the same thing in the second year.

In May/June of the third year you can cut a little—but only a little—asparagus for the kitchen.   A very sharp, short-bladed, stiff knife, or a curved pruning knife is best for this.   Cut well below the soil surface, by touch, not at the surface.   And take care to keep close to the shoot you are cutting with the knife, for you can easily damage brittle young buds which have not yet shown above ground.   It is very difficult to tell you how much asparagus you can safely cut without harming the plants; some plants will be more vigorous than others.   Don't cut from weak ones in the early years.   Cutting starts in May.   I should not take more than one shoot per plant in year 3; two in year 4.   After that you may cut all the shoots which appear until 20 June in a year of normal weather.   Then stop cutting.

Every year the ridges will sink a little and ultimately the asparagus rows will be level with the general surface.   If you can spare the compost, give an extra dressing to the area after cutting off the dead 'fern' in late autumn.

Asparagus is what botanists call a dioecious species.   That means that the male and female flowers do not grow together on any one plant, *ie* there are male and female plants.   Ideally an asparagus bed should have only male plants.   But there are, as a rule, female plants among them.   These set seed and so you are sure to get asparagus seedlings in the bed.   (And all over the garden, for birds eat the berries).   Treat these as weeds; they tend to produce only 'sprue'.

Pests and diseases   None of any significance.

Aubergine   See p. 99.

Capsicums (*Sweet Peppers,* or *Green Peppers*)   See p. 99.

Cardoon is very closely related to globe artichoke but is culti-vated for its blanched leaf stalks and leaf mid-ribs.   Prepare trenches as for *celery* (see p. 44).   Raise the plant from seed sown in a nursery bed under glass or cloches in March, for planting out in May, 20 inches apart in rows 40 inches apart.   Keep rows hoed free of weeds and the inter-rows roto-vated, or hoed if you are using them for a catch crop of lettuce, radish etc.   Irrigate in dry weather.   Nothing else need be done until mid-September; then, waiting for a dry spell, draw the leaves together into a bundle, tie them like that with raffia or string, and over each 'bundle' slip a tube of black polythene and bind it in place.   Then earth-up as for celery. (see p. 45).

93

Chard is often used instead of Cardoon, but I use it here to mean Swiss Chard which is a kind of beet, rather like spinach beet, producing large green leaves on very thick, juicy white stalks and midribs. The stalks and midribs are used like asparagus; the green part of the leaf, torn away from the midrib, like spinach. Sow the seed in drills 1 inch deep and 20 inches apart, in a fine tilth in April. Thin seedlings to nine inches apart.

Chinese cabbage, or **Petsai,** is a superlative vegetable which has become known in Britain since the rise in the numbers of Chinese immigrants from Hong Kong, and of Chinese restaurants. Like our own cabbage it belongs to the genus *Brassica* but not to the same species. It looks like a very large, dense and heavy Cos lettuce, and can, in fact, be used as salad as well as cooked like our own cabbage; the cabbage flavour (and cooking smell) is milder.

A first sowing can be made in May and successional sowings in June and July. Cultivate exactly as if you were growing *lettuce* (see p. 46).

Chicory   See *Witloof* and, incidentally, *Endive*.

Cress   See *Mustard and Cress* (p. 95).

Cucumber (see also p. 100) can be grown in the open as well as under glass. Suitable varieties are Burpee Hybrid and Carter's Greenline. Sow the seeds, one to a three-inch pot, in a greenhouse, a cold frame or under a cloche, in April. Keep the seedlings watered. Harden-off during the middle two weeks of May. Plant out at the end of May 20 inches apart in rows 20 inches apart. Keep free of weeds by hoeing and rotovating. Irrigate during dry spells.

Endive (and *Chicory*)   There is a confusing diversity of names: endive, chicory, witloof. Here we shall use two names: endive, for the curly-leaved salad; witloof (p. 102) for blanched smooth leaved salad which can also be cooked as a vegetable—in fact, many people think it is better cooked than raw.

Although very useful in the second half of the year since it is hardier than lettuce, I doubt if endive is worth growing during that part of the year when lettuce is at its best. So make a first sowing in early July. For sowing and cultivation, see *lettuce*

(p. 46).   But, when the plants are full grown, start blanching.   You do this by gathering the leaves together and tying them in a bundle so that light is excluded from the inside ones, which will remain pale green and tender.   Do a few plants at a time as and when you will want to use them.   Two 10 yard rows will carry you through the winter.

The unblanched outer leaves are bitter and coarse, but the blanched inner leaves have a good flavour and remain crisp when served in a French dressing.

Fennel is the vegetable or salad which the travelled reader will have had in Italy as *Finocchio dolce*.   It can be grown here but expect some failures of plants to swell into good sized bulbous stem bases—the best of the edible part.   The texture is the same as celery; the taste is aniseed.   The crispest inner part makes good salad, the outer part is better cooked.

A first sowing should be made in early or mid May in drills 1 inch deep and 20 inches apart in trenches as for *celery* (p. 45).   If you want a succession, go on sowing at 20 day intervals until mid-August.   Thin the seedlings to 9 or 10 inches apart.   Do not start earthing up until the plants are large and the bases of the stems are becoming bulbous.   Then earth-up as for celery.

Kohl Rabi is not exactly a root vegetable, the edible part being a swollen stem, just above soil level, of what is a kind of cabbage plant.   Sow in April in shallow drills 20 inches apart.   Harvest in July.   A second sowing in May can be harvested in August.   Kohl rabi which are allowed to grow larger than a big orange are not worth eating, so harvest when they are quite small, about eleven or twelve weeks after sowing the seeds.

Mangetout or **Sugar Peas**   You eat the whole pod; pick them before you can see the swelling of the peas in the pod, otherwise they will be stringy.   Grow them, sowing seed from March onwards, exactly like ordinary peas (p. 49).   A good variety is Dwarf Sweet Green.   As the plants grow to 3 feet, some support is necessary.

Mustard and cress salad is grown from seed at any time of the year under glass, and in late spring and summer in the open.   Fill some shallow boxes or trays with fine, sterilized soil pressed firm and level with a piece of wood.   Half of them will be used for cress and half for mustard. Sow the cress seed thickly and evenly over the surface and press it into the soil with a short piece of plank. Keep moist and cover, until germination, with sheets of cardboard or thick brown paper. Remove it as soon as the seeds germinate. Three days after the cress has germinated sow the mustard seed in the same way. The two will be ready at the same time.

Mushrooms are not difficult to grow, but you need a shed, a greenhouse or some other covered place where a temperature of between 55° and 60°F. can easily be maintained. Mushrooms do not require a high temperature, in fact they will not grow if the temperature is above 68°F. They need not be grown in the dark, and are perfectly happy in ordinary daylight.

The classic compost for mushrooms was made by fermenting a mixture of horse manure and straw but this is no longer necessary (though still, of course, a very good way of doing it). There is now a material called Boost, made by Messrs Darlington, which will reduce straw to the right condition for growing mushrooms. A 6 lb pack of Boost applied to a 1 cwt bale of straw will produce about 6 cubic feet of compost. Spread 6 inches deep this gives a surface of 12 square feet, a reasonable size for the amateur's mushroom bed. Spawn can be bought in various forms. One of the easiest to use is Grain Spawn (prepared by Dobies of Llangollen).

It does not matter where you make the bed for mushrooms so long as it is somewhere where the temperature can be maintained at about 60°F. The compost should be made firm and level and the Grain Spawn scattered on it and lightly covered with compost. The bed must be kept moist but not actually wet: it is as well to do any necessary watering with warm water but it should not exceed 65°F.

Pea, Asparagus 'Asparagus Peas' are neither a kind of asparagus nor a kind of pea. But if picked and cooked at the right moment they are a palatable change from the the commoner vegetables. The species is an annual and grows about 18 inches tall. Sow the seeds 4 inches apart in 1 inch drills 20 inches apart, in early May—and, if you want a succession, again in June. The seedlings should be irrigated in dry weather. Pick the pods for cooking when they are not more than 1½ inches long. You cook the whole pod.

Pumpkin   Cultivation as for *Marrows* (p. 47).

Salsify is a hardy biennial plant: you eat the long, fleshy root and, in Spring, the young leaf shoots.   Sow the seeds in 1 inch deep drills 20 inches apart in April and as soon as the seedlings can be handled thin them out so that the plants are seven or eight inches apart.   No other work excepting the usual hoeing and rotovating to keep the weeds down is required.   The roots are ready for use in late October and can, like parsnips, be dug up as required right through the winter.   Any which remain in spring will send up tender and succulent shoots which are wholesome and palatable.

Scorzonera is another root vegetable, very like salsify excepting that the skin of the roots is black.   Cultivation is as for salsify but you eat only the roots.   Russian Giant is a good variety.

Tomatoes (For tomatoes under glass, see p. 101).   Sow the seed in boxes or trays of sterilized John Innes Compost in April under glass.   If you have no source of heat in the greenhouse or no greenhouse at all, you can start the seeds off on the window sill of a warm living room.

When the seedlings are 1½ inches tall, carefully prick them out into 3 inch pots, one to a pot, using John Innes No. 3 Compost.   Keep them well watered and under glass or indoors all the time until the end of April.   Then begin to harden them off by putting them outside during fine weather, though at first you will have to bring them in at night.   They will not stand even a touch of frost.

In mid May prepare for planting out by hammering stout wooden stakes into the ground at intervals of 20 inches along the row chosen for growing tomatoes.   If you are growing more than one row, the rows should be 20 inches apart.   You'll need stakes 4 feet long, so that there are 3 feet of stake above the surface after they have been driven in.

Plant out the young tomato plants during the last week in May or the first week in June—it must not be done until there is no danger of frost.   Water the plants in and then mulch with compost an inch or so deep.

As the tomatoes grow you must:

(1)   Tie them to the stakes, firmly enough to keep them

97

upright but loosely enough to give plenty of room for growth of girth in the stem.   A new tie at every six inches.

(2)   Pinch out the little side shoots which develop in the leaf axils.   This is important; if these branches are allowed to grow the plants will be unwieldy and fruit development will be checked.

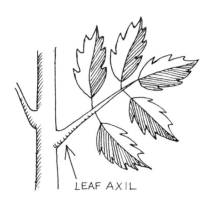

LEAF AXIL

(3)   Keep the plants well watered in dry weather and free from weeds at all times.

(4)   As soon as four trusses (clusters) of fruit are set, pinch out the growing tip of the plants.   It is useless to try for more than 4 trusses on tomato plants in the open.   (Under glass it is quite another matter).

(5)   Continue to pinch out side shoots and tip shoots as fast as they develop.   Tomatoes are incredibly vigorous plants and hard to keep well in hand.

(6)   As the lower leaves begin to turn yellowish, cut them off and put them on the compost heap.   Once the tomatoes on the highest and last truss have reached full size, the plants will probably be bare of leaves excepting at the top, but this does not matter.

You may like to try a technique of my own for getting a longer season of tomatoes.   It is a gamble, because it only works well if the autumn is fine and warm.   Instead of pinching it out, allow the very first side shoot on each plant (but *only that one*) to grow till it is 5 or 6 inches long.   Then cut it out from the leaf axil with a sharp knife and plant it in a 5 inch pot of compost, under glass but shaded from direct sun.   Keep the soil moist at

98

all times.   The cuttings will root within a few days, and once rooted can be hardened off and planted out.   Let two trusses, three at most, set before pinching out the tip growth.

There are some tomato varieties for cultivation in the open, known as bush-tomatoes.   They do not require either staking or pinching out, but the ground round them should be covered with a layer of clean straw to keep the fruits clean and dry.   A good variety of this kind is The Amateur.

There are a number of vegetable/salad crops which are either best grown under glass or can *only* be grown under glass: that is, in a greenhouse with some means of heating occasionally, to exclude frost and keep the temperature above 45°F early and late in the year.   Here they are:

Aubergine, or **Egg Plant** are, like the *capsicums* (below) related to the tomato, (all three are members of the family *Solanaceae* to which also belong tobacco and a number of poisonous plants including Henbane and Deadly Nightshade.)

Sow the seeds under glass and with artificial heat in February, in a box or tray of John Innes Compost.   When the seedlings are about 1½ inches tall prick them out into 3 inch pots and when they are about 6 inches tall, into 7 inch pots filled with rich compost.   Keep the pots well watered, syringe the foliage as often as you can with clean water to discourage the Red Spider mite, and about once a week add a small dose of liquid fertilizer to their water.

Artificial heating will not be needed after May.

At the time of transplanting to 7 inch pots, pinch out the growing tip of each plant.   This will make them produce branches.   Allow only four to grow, pinching out any others.   You should get one fruit to each branch.   If more fruits 'set' either remove all but one on each branch, or double the fertilizer feed frequency to twice a week.

Capsicum or **Green Peppers** are as easy to grow in a greenhouse as tomatoes.   Sow the seed in March in a box or tray which should be kept near a source of heat.   When the seedlings are about 6/7 inches tall, prick them out, into John Innes Compost in 3 inch pots, one per pot.   Keep them warm and watered.   When they are four or five inches tall, transfer

99

them into 7 inch pots filled with rich compost. From May onwards they will do very well in an unheated greenhouse or if you like to put them outside, under cloches. They are less prone to branching than tomatoes and, shorter and sturdier, do not usually require staking. A small dose of liquid fertilizer in their water once every ten days will produce large fruits.

Pests Capsicums are very prone to attack by the greenhouse red spider mite. The best way to discourage this creature is not to confine watering to the soil, but to syringe the foliage as often as you can. A really bad attack is best dealt with by fumigation with a sulphur vaporizer.

Cucumber Not the outdoor, or 'Ridge' cucumber, but the long 'English' cucumber gives its best results at greenhouse temperatures much higher than most amateurs can afford to maintain and at a humidity so high that it is difficult to grow other crops in the same house. However, very good results are possible in much less than optimum conditions, either in greenhouses, frames or under cloches. Here is a method which works well:

(1) Sow cucumber seed one per pot in 3 inch pots of John Innes Compost in April. If your greenhouse is not heated, put the pots, well watered, into a cardboard box, the whole box into a polythene bag, sealed by knotting and tying, and bring it into a warm room. Let the seedlings develop two or three good leaves before you move the whole thing into the greenhouse in mid May. Admit fresh air to them after a few days.

(2) Across all or part of one end of the greenhouse fix in place one or two 1 inch planks, on edge, to create a transom 12 inches deep, 24 inches from the end of the house. Cover the bottom of the area so enclosed with drainage material—stones, broken crocks, clinker and then fill it to a depth of 9 inches with compost. Behind this bed you must fix rigid plastic trellis against the inside of the end of the greenhouse to a height of five feet. Don't plant the young cucumbers until the soil of this bed has had time to warm up. Ideally, it should be over 65°F.

(3) Plant the cucumber plants at intervals of 20 inches. You should be able to do this without disturbing the soil-and-root ball by tapping it out of the pots in one piece.

(4) In about 2 weeks if the greenhouse is warm enough new roots will appear from the cucumber stems on the surface of the

soil. Cover them with compost, dress the surface with 8 ounces of fine bonemeal per 10 square feet of surface, and water it in. Whenever you water cucumbers, spray the foliage with clean water.

(5) As the plants grow, tie the main shoot to the trellis so that it is growing vertically; and its side shoots so that they are kept horizontal. When the main stem is 5 feet long, stop it by pinching-out. The cucumbers will be borne on the side shoots and sub-laterals.

Diseases: there are a number. A bacterial canker attacks the base of the stems if the soil surface is too wet and cold. You can reduce the danger of this by mounding up the soil at the base of each plant to draw water away from it; and by dusting the bases of the cucumber plant stems with a copper-lime dust.

Leaves and parts of stems turn yellow, become very dry and brittle, turning to brown. This is a fungus disease. Treatment is to burn badly infected leaves and spray the plants with a sulphur-based fungicide. This will also eliminate Cucumber-Mildew and check another disease, Gummosis. Much trouble can be avoided by growing a disease-resistant variety of which there are several.

Cucumbers can also be grown in frames and under cloches. For cultivation see *melons,* (p. 121).

Tomatoes Raising of plants from seed has been described on p. 97. For plants to be grown under glass, sow the seed in March. If the greenhouse has a solid floor you can either make a temporary bed as described above for cucumbers. Or you can plant one to a 9 inch pot of good compost. In either case use one of the special tomato fertilizers like Fisons, ICI and others, when watering, once a week. These proprietary fertilizers are useful for the necessary feeding of pot-grown tomatoes. For quantities and frequency of feeding follow the instructions on the package. If the greenhouse has a soil bottom, you can plant directly into the soil, but if you do so year after year the soil becomes 'tomato sick'. This means that you will have to dig out the soil every other year and bring in fresh soil from the garden.

The tomatoes will need supports—either bamboo canes, or strings stretched from a peg at the base of the plants to nails in the roof rafters of the greenhouse.

Pinch out side-shoots as soon as they appear. A few may be

allowed to grow big enough to be cut off and used as cuttings (see p. 98).   Give plenty of ventilation in warm weather, do not overwater, especially when the plants are young, and in heated greenhouses syringe the foliage from time to time.

Under glass you can allow as many trusses of fruit as the height of the greenhouse leaves room for; in practice this will probably not exceed seven.   You will find, by the way, that at the end of the season you will be left with some fully-grown but still green tomatoes both out-of-doors and in the greenhouse.   They can be ripened in the house, on a window sill, or used to make green tomato chutney.

Witloof is Chicory grown as a forced winter salad.   It is troublesome to grow but you may wish to try it.

Refer back to *endive*.   Grow a row of chicory in the same way but don't cut it, just leave it alone, except for hoeing until early November.   Dig up the carrot-like roots, cut off the leaves at the top and pinch-out any side shoots.   Cut the root tips, so that all the roots are about 10 inches long.   Store them by burying them in sand in a shed where frost cannot get at them.

You will need some boxes at least a foot deep.   Fill them with soil and plant the roots, as supplies are required, 3 inches apart and with one inch still above the soil which is moist.   Cover with an inverted box of the same size, and put the box or boxes into a shed or greenhouse where the temperature can be maintained at between 50°F. and 55°F.

Shoots fit for eating will take about 4 weeks to grow.   By drawing on your store of roots and making such a planting once a week you can have witloof from late December well into April.

CHAPTER 7   FRUIT DICTIONARY

The garden, being enlarged from 300 square yards to twice that area, or at all events enlarged, the 300 yard basic unit will still be managed as a continuing cycle of planting and cropping as described in Part 1.   But a part of the additional area we are now considering must be managed rather differently, because we now have to deal not only with annual crop plants, but with perennials, like asparagus, and shrubs and trees, like raspberries and apples, which last up to a lifetime or more.

As, moreover, the entire area is still to be cultivated intensively, the fruit trees will not, in fact, be trees in the ordinary meaning of the word; by growing those kinds which can be dwarfed, as dwarfs and keeping them to a restricted shape, we make it much easer to interplant with vegetables or with such annual fruit crops as melons.

In Chapter 8 I describe a plan for intensive cropping of this second unit of your food garden.   You can, of course, adapt and modify it to suit yourself.   Before we come to that, however, it will be best to describe how to grow the fruit crops we are adding to the list.

For the purpose of the kind of garden management I have in mind, I am in what follows, suggesting the revival of techniques developed by the house of Thomas Rivers & Sons in the last century.

Apples   *Preparation*   I am assuming, once again, that we are working with a 10 yard garden row.   It will be easy enough for you to adapt this up or down, according to the size and shape of your garden.   A single ten yard row will accommodate 5 or 6 apple trees.   I think you should have 10 apple trees: so, two rows.   They should be six feet apart.

Since there are 2 rows, you will require 8 stout (3 x 3 in or 4 x 4 in) oak or chestnut posts 4 feet long, sharply pointed at one end, and treated with a copper preservative.   Hammer these into the ground so that 30 inches are left above the ground.   Stretch galvanised iron wire absolutely taut, at 9 inches, 18 inches and 27 inches from the surface of the soil, so that you now have 4 structures like this:

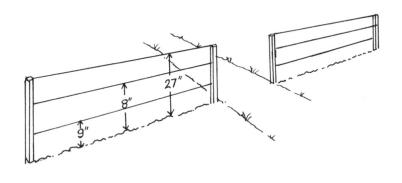

Fork over the soil which has been trodden down by the work.   Preparation is now complete.

Buying apple trees   The sort of plants you want would be described as 'maidens without feathers grafted of MV No. 11'.

'Maidens' are young trees consisting of a single shoot of the scion variety (usually 3 or 4 feet tall) growing on a root of the required rootstock variety.   'Feathers' = young side shoots.   'MV 11' = the number designating the rootstock you require in order that the trees shall be dwarfish.

Varieties   There is absolutely no point in the amateur planting any but the best varieties.   Indifferent varieties are just as troublesome to grow.   Many of the newer varieties have been bred for such commercially valuable qualities as ease and robustness in handling and marketing rather than flavour.   We need more than one variety to get a good 'set' of fruit; cross pollination is essential.   Furthermore by planting several varieties you can get a succession of crops.   Here is a suggested list:

James Grieve or Worcester Pearmain for eating in September and October.

Cox's Orange Pippin for eating in November and December.

Orleans Reinette for eating January and February, or Tydeman's Late Orange.

Winston for keeping till March.

Charles Ross to use as a cooking apple (because Bramley's Seedling, the best cooker is awkward to grow as a dwarf, trained tree).

So your order to the nurseryman will be something like this:

Two each of James Grieve, Tydeman's Late Orange, Orleans Reinette, Winston.

Three Cox's Orange Pippin.

One Charles Ross.

All maidens without feathers grafted on MV 11.

Just a note about that MV 11. It is only one of several possible dwarfing stocks. If you have a good local fruit tree nursery, they may recommend another. But emphasize that you want dwarfing, not semi-dwarfing stock. And do *not* accept the stock called 'Type 1X'. Place the order in summer for delivery in November.

Planting   Dig holes at 30 inches from the end of each row and at intervals thereafter of 5 feet along the row. These holes should be wide enough to take the roots of your young trees, or the root ball if container-grown, and as deep as necessary to get the soil mark on the shoot, or the container surface, level with the general surface of the soil.

Fruit trees must be planted very firmly indeed. Put the soil ball, or, if not container-grown, spread the roots, in the hole, fill in with earth and then tread it firm with your heel, all round the tree using the full weight of your body. Repeat this until you can no longer tread the soil lower than the surrounding surface. If you're really thorough you will even get a baulk of timber and pound the soil hard, though not until there's enough of it over the roots to protect them from bruising or breaking.

When planting is complete, take your secateurs, a small pot of lead paint, and a paint brush and carefully examine each young tree. What you are looking for is the three buds nearest to the bottom wire, *ie* about 9 inches from the ground.

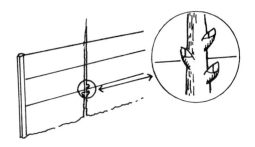

Cut off the shoot above bud A, making a slanting cut like this:

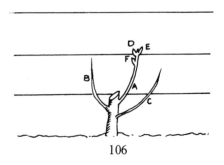

Paint the cut surface.   Lightly hoe the whole surface.

Year 1   Spring: mulch each tree with compost mixed with half a handful of bonemeal.   Bud A begins to grow.   When it is well above the second wire so that there are three buds below the growing tip fairly near to the second wire which is 18 inches above the ground, pinch out the growing tip.   We'll call the three buds near the second wire, D, E and F.

Buds B and C will already be growing, but not as vigorously as Bud A.   But after that pinching-out they will grow faster.   You now have something like this:

106

D, E and F begin to grow. As a result, at the end of the growing season, and if all other growth is restricted to three or four leaves by pinching-out, you will have something like this:

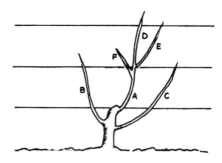

Bend down B, C, E, and F and bend over D to get this:

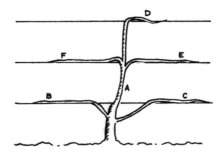

and tie the shoots in place.

Year 2 Spring: mulch each tree with compost enriched with half a handful of bonemeal. A bud near D will begin to grow: let it; the tip buds of the horizontals will begin to grow; let them. The buds along the horizontals will begin to grow; let each one produce five leaves and then pinch out the growing tips: these will then form what are called 'fruit spurs'.   At the end of the season you will have something like this:

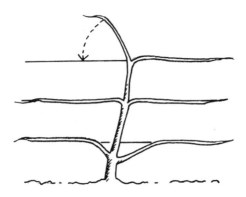

Bend down top spur and tie it to the wire.

Year 3   You will get some flowers and in due course, fruit.   The tips of the six horizontals continue to grow.   And side shoots on all of them.   Pinch out the growing tips after five leaves have developed.   Continue to do this throughout the season.

   Now it will be obvious that as growth continues the horizontals of neighbouring trees will overlap.   Let them do so by six inches and then stop them by pinching out.   At the season's end you have something like this:

Year 4   We are now going to join all the trees together to create a single, rigid structure.   The tips of the horizontal branches of each tree now overlap each other by about six inches.   In March cut them back until the overlap is two or three inches like this:

Now, using a very sharp knife cut them like this:

Now you'll need a roll of insulating tape.   Join the overlapping ends together like this

and bandage them tightly and thoroughly together so that the joint is well covered.   The branches will grow together to form an integral mass of tissue.   One year later you will be able to remove the posts and wire because these trees will be self-supporting.

The horizontal branches will continue to produce side shoots; allow each one to grow to five leaves long.   Then in December when you do the small amount of pruning necessary with this type of *espalier* tree, shorten each back with the secateurs to only 3 buds long.   These side shoots so treated will turn into fruit-bearing spurs.

The advantages of this kind of *espalier* are manifold.   There is much less winter pruning and it is much easier to get at.   Pest control spraying is very much easier.   The fruit is of superior quality.   Vegetable crops can be grown between the rows.

Pests and diseases   Apple trees are unfortunately affected by numerous pests and diseases and these must be controlled.   It should be noted that trees growing in fertile soil, mulched with reinforced compost every year, kept free of weeds by good cultivation with hoe and rotovator, are much less prone to diseases and pests than neglected apple trees.

Aphids: seven species attack apple trees.   Fortunately they can all be controlled by killing their eggs which over-winter on

109

the trees. You do this by *thoroughly* spraying the trees in mid-winter with Tar-oil winter wash or one of the other winter-washes. If you nevertheless get an attack of aphis, spray with Malathion, wetting both sides of the leaves.

Capsid Buds can badly scar and spoil the fruit. A thorough tar-oil wash in winter kills their eggs. Eggs which survive hatch in April. Spray thoroughly with Malathion.

Winter washing with tar-oil tends to control half a dozen other, less damaging, insect pests. Some are also destroyed by the spraying to control fungus diseases which should be carried out as a matter of routine. The worst of these is:

Scab The symptoms are brown and black splotches on the leaves; round black spots and blotches on the fruitlets; cracks and blisters on young shoots. Scab is more prevalent in wet counties than in dry ones, and in wet than dry weather. The disease can be prevented by the following routine:

(1) When the flower buds are just about to open, that is are just showing a glimpse of pink, spray thoroughly with a solution of Lime-Sulphur at the strength recommended by the makers. It is about 1 part lime-sulphur to 30 parts of water.

(2) Spray again as soon as the flower petals have fallen, using a much weaker solution, about 1 in 75 parts of water.

(3) Spray again 3 weeks after spray number 2, and the solution to be 1 in 100 parts of water.

Warning: Stronger solution will seriously damage certain varieties, notably Cox's Orange Pippin.

This lime-sulphur spraying routine will do a lot to control some insect pests as well, and furthermore it will do something to reduce the incidence of *canker* which in one form attacks the wood of the trees and in another the fruit. The fruit attack is called Brown Rot and may not be the same; nobody seems to be quite sure. If, lime-sulphur routine notwithstanding, Scab occurs, you will find it as a small, oval depression in the bark which steadily increases in size; as it does so, the central area flakes and crumbles away. In time, if you get it, the canker circles the bark and kills the twig or branch. So you must stop it before it gets the chance. Small twigs attacked: cut off down to clean, healthy tissue and paint over with white-lead paint. Larger branches or trunks: with a very sharp knife cut out the infected area down to clean, healthy tissue and paint over the wound with white lead paint.

All this sounds alarming: but if you are meticulous with your winter-wash and your lime-sulphur routines, you should not get much trouble.

Apricots are, in my experience, difficult to succeed with in Britain but still some professional and many amateur growers do get good crops. Use exactly the same technique as described under *cherries* (below) but instead of trying to shape your own trees, buy 3-year-old fan-trained specimens to start with. For the summer pruning technique follow the directions given under *plums*. For *Pests and diseases*, too, see *plums*. If you do succeed with this fruit and your trees set heavy crops of apricots, they should be thinned to a final spacing of 5 or 6 inches, like *peaches* (see below).

The varieties most likely to succeed in Britain are Early Moor Park and Hemskerk.

Berries, *ie* Blackberries, Loganberries, Wineberries etc (but see p. 127 for raspberries). For these you require a structure similar to that erected for espalier apples but 5 feet tall and with 6 wires at 9 inch intervals.

Year 1 Plant the berry plants in November 8 feet apart in rows 6 feet apart. Cut back the canes to a plump bud 15 inches or so from the ground.

The root will produce a number of canes. As they grow tie them or twist them onto the wires to form a pattern which looks like this:

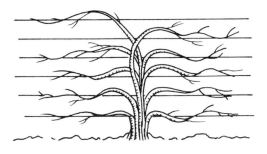

Ten canes will be sufficient. Cut out any more which appear, at the base or below soil level.

Year 2 In spring, mulch with compost and bonemeal at two handfuls per plant. While last year's canes are bearing fruit, new ones will grow from the root.   Allow ten to grow, cutting out any surplus ones at or below soil level.   As these new canes grow tie them in a loose bundle and to the wire, vertically.   As soon as fruiting is over and all the fruit has been picked, cut out the old canes at or below soil level and burn them.   Then sort out the new canes and train and tie them in place for *Year 3*.   Repeat this process every year.

Pests and diseases   None that you need worry about—or can do anything about if they should occur which is not likely.

Cherries   Here, when considering the whole intensive plan of the garden, I am in a difficulty.   There are no dwarfing rootstocks for cherry trees; standard cherry trees cannot be planted less than 40 feet apart; and nothing but grass can be grown under them, though you can keep chickens or even sheep on the grass.   There is a way of growing cherries as single cordons but it entails double-grafting, an art which nurserymen can no longer afford to practice.

I am, however, very reluctant to exclude cherries from our garden.   Among the most delicious of fruits, the great Kentish orchards are being run down and grubbed up owing to the cost of picking the fruit and the last defender of this, as of other manifestations of civilized living, is the amateur gardener.   I therefore propose to say something about the cultivation of fan-trained cherry trees.   It was usual to grow them on a wall but they could just as well be grown in the open on a wire structure like that recommended above for blackberries.

Varieties   The first thing will be to persuade a nurseryman to graft some cherry trees for you not as for standards, at 7 feet from the ground, but at a few inches above soil level; and then let you have them as 'maidens' (see p. 104).   We have 5 yards of room each side of our central path.   We need only four trees, but as cross-pollination is essential there must be more than one variety.   I suggest two Biggareau Napoleon, one Early Rivers and one Waterloo.

Planting   Now; you'll need a post and wire structure like the one used for *berries* (above).   Construct two rows with 10 feet between them—that space will be needed for vegetable crops; or asparagus beds; or strawberry beds.   Plant in November, one little tree to the centre of each 5 yard row.   Plant, as in the case of apples, very firmly indeed, heeling and pounding the

112

soil round the root.   Then cut off the single shoot which is your young cherry tree to six buds above the graft scar (a sort of bulge in the stem).   When you have time during the winter, provide yourself with two dozen very long, thin, bamboo canes.   Tie or wire to the wire structure like this:

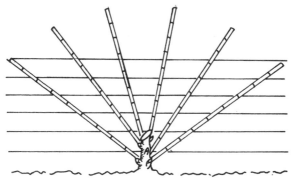

As, in the following year, the six buds of your juvenile cherry tree grow, tie them to those canes.   When side-shoots start to grow on these six main shoots, let them make five or six leaves and then pinch out the growing tips of the side-shoots.   What we aim to do is to make a cherry tree which, instead of a trunk and branches, has six trunks and a mass of fruiting spurs.   The problem is to restrict the growth of a plant which wants to grow much bigger than we want it to be.   So: no mulch, no fertilizer.   Garden hygiene requires that we keep weeds hoed down, but nothing else.

At the end of the growing season which gives you the above fan pattern, move the canes and branches so that the final shape of the trees will be like this:

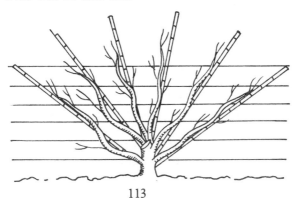

113

Pests and diseases   From experience I should say that the only troubles the amateur gardener need worry about are bacterial die-back and Silver Leaf Disease.   There are others—a lot of them—but they are not common.   The risk from Silver Leaf can be reduced by never cutting—*ie* pruning—the trees between the end of August and the end of March; and by spraying with a copper-lime fungicide at leaf-fall.   The disease is due to a fungus parasite and the most noticeable symptom is a curious silvery look which mars the green of the leaves.   The same preventatives will also reduce the risk of die-back.

Currants, Black   Plant the young bushes 6 feet apart in rows 8 feet apart.   As soon as planting is completed, in November or December, cut them down to ground level, hoe the soil and rotovate between the rows.   In March mulch with compost reinforced with one handful of bonemeal and an ounce of sulphate of ammonia per bush.

Black Currants bear their fruit on *new* wood.   Pruning therefore consists in cutting out a proportion of the old wood every autumn after the fruit is over, to make room for new shoots from the root.

The annual dressing of compost and fertiliser (see p. 27) will be adequate manuring.

Varieties recommended are: (Early) Boskoop Giant, (mid-season) Wellington XXX, (late) Baldwin.

Pests and diseases   Six species of Aphids are parasitic on currants.   As all of them leave their over-wintering eggs on the bushes, very thorough winter-washing with tar-oil (See apples, p. 110) will give control.   As some of these aphids spend a part of their life on various weeds, very clean cultivation of the black currant rows is essential.

Big Bud mite is a serious pest of black currants.   The symptom is a swelling of the buds in summer, to an abnormal size.   Apart from the direct damage done by this mite, it is the vector (carrier) of a virus disease called reversion.   It can be controlled by thorough syringing in spring, when the young leaves are the size of a 5-penny piece, with lime-sulphur—1 pint to every 5 gallons of water.

'Reversion', a virus disease, can be troublesome, usually on old bushes.   The symptom to watch for is a deformity of the leaves.   (See over).   Reverted bushes should be dug up and

114

burnt.   Control of Big Bud Mite reduces the risk of Reversion.

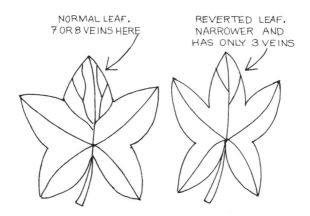

NORMAL LEAF.
7 OR 8 VEINS HERE

REVERTED LEAF.
NARROWER AND
HAS ONLY 3 VEINS

Currants, Red and White.   White currant is simply a variety
of red currant and is treated identically.   Plant 6 feet apart in
rows 8 feet apart.

Red and white currants, unlike black currants, bear their
fruit on *old* wood.   And whereas black currants are grown as
'stools', with new shoots continuously arising from the roots,
red and white currants should be grown on a leg, like a small
tree.

Pruning: in February cut back all side shoots to 3 buds and cut
back the tips of main shoots by about 1 inch.

Manuring and cultivation: as for black currants.

Varieties: (Early) White Versailles, (mid-season) Laxton No. 1,
(late) Wilson's Longbunch.

Pests and diseases are less troublesome than on black currants
and need not worry the amateur gardener, but a tar-oil wash
(See *apples*) is worth while.

Damsons: see *plums*.

Figs succeed well in Britain where they have been grown for
over 1,500 years.   Planted in deep, light to medium, fertile
soil, their roots, unrestricted, stimulate such lush growth that
little or no fruit is borne.   For healthy trees and good crops,
short, stubby, hard wood growth is needed and this is best
obtained by root restriction.   A 5 yard row (in full sun) will

accommodate 3 fig trees. Plant a full row (10 yards) or more if you like, but for the amateur gardener something more modest is safer. If the sub-soil of your garden is heavy clay, you can risk planting without special preparation. Otherwise you must undertake a small building-worker's job, or get someone to do it for you.

Preparation With their centres five feet apart, dig out 3 neatly rectangular holes one yard cube—*ie* 3' x 3' x 3'. Line the sides either with bricks laid on the narrow, not on the broad side, with cement and sand (1-3 Mix) mortar; or with two inch walls of concrete. Into the sub-soil bottom of the pits, hammer five or six short, stout, round pegs (*eg* cut from an old broomstick). Pour in and level a floor of concrete 3 inches thick. As soon as it is beginning to harden, pull out the wooden pegs. That will leave drainage holes. When the concrete has set, cover the bottom of each pit with a two or three inch layer of broken brick, shards, pebbles, broken bottles etc., to ensure good drainage. Now refill the pits with the soil you took from them, stamping it down as firm and hard as you can; keep the best of the top-soil for the top, of course. Plant in November—or at any time if you're using container-grown young trees—one fig tree at the centre of each pit. The annual dressings of compost will be all the manuring you will ever need.

Pruning Do it in May. First cut out any dead wood, making sure that you cut back to healthy wood unstained by the brown marks of die-back. Try to cut to an outside bud. In the same way, cut off any dead tip-buds. The only other pruning will be to shape the tree if it grows lop-sided, or badly balanced. Again cut to an outside bud. The trees will bleed a white latex. Don't worry about that, it will not harm the trees. Strong growing shoots should be pruned back to seven or eight leaves in September.

Irrigation If the month of June is dry, the fig-trees should be kept very thoroughly watered to prevent them dropping too many fruitlets.

Varieties The two most reliable: Brown Turkey and Brunswick.

Pests and diseases: none you need worry about.

Gooseberries For directions for planting, manuring, cultivation, pruning and pest-control, please see under *currants, red* (p.

116

115), for gooseberries require exactly the same treatment. But there is a way of growing gooseberries and red
currants (also apples and pears, but not black currants) which
makes them easier to handle and economises space because you
can grow catch crops between the rows. This form of
gooseberry bush is called a cordon. A cordon is a bush or tree
restricted to a single stem and so pruned that side shoots are
transformed into fruiting spurs. If you are going to grow
gooseberries as cordons, don't buy bushes, buy young cordons. As not many nurseries sell them in that form, I shall
name one that does: Thomas Rivers & Sons, Sawbridgeworth,
Herts.

Preparation Erect a structure identical with that described for
berries (p. 111). Now, at intervals of 18 inches, wire to the
wires of that structure, long, thin bamboo canes at an angle of
30° to the vertical, until you have a row which looks like this:

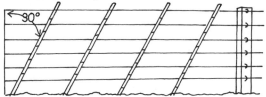

In November plant a young cordon gooseberry bush at the
foot of each cane and tie it to the cane. You will need 20
cordons per 10 yard row. If you want more than one row, put
them six feet apart and use the space between for vegetable and
salad crops. Manuring will consist of the annual dressings of
compost reinforced with bonemeal (one ounce per cordon,
hoed in).

Pruning The only part of the cordons which is allowed to grow
without restriction until it reaches to the top of the cane is the
tip growth. For the rest, pruning should be done in the
growing season, with the thumb-nail—*ie* any side shoots should
be pinched out above the third leaf, to form more fruit
spurs. If any do get away, shorten them back to three buds in
winter.

Varieties Leveller. Yellow fruit of very good flavour and an
enormous cropper. Whinham's Industry. Heavy cropping
variety. The fruit is red when ripe.

Grapes (See also Chapter 10 for *vineyards*). The grapes
which succeed in the open in England, and then only in the

117

south, are for the most part more suitable for wine-making than for eating.   There are, however, some of dessert quality which do well on a warm south-facing wall or wooden fence; and a number which do well in a greenhouse.   Finally, there are the best, which can only be grown to perfection in a heated greenhouse.

Readers who wish to try grapes in open rows should refer to Chapter Ten.   Here I shall confine myself to grapes on walls and grapes under glass.

Wall grapes   The wall should first be equipped with a system of taut galvanized iron wires at 12 inch intervals from top to bottom, held well away from the surface by long vine-eyes screwed or hammered into the brick.   If there is good garden soil at the foot of the wall, no special preparation is required.   Vines don't like dense clay, but do like brick rubble.   Grape vines bear their fruits on the young wood of the previous season's growth only.   So your object must be to produce a permanent structure of old wood on which new wood will grow and bear each year.

Varieties   A number of vines will succeed on walls in this country but the three usually suggested are Black Hamburgh, Royal Muscadine and Buckland Sweetwater.   In my experience Black Hamburgh often fails to ripen and Buckland Sweetwater has no flavour.   I suggest therefore, Royal Muscadine which is the English name for the *Chasselas doré de Fontainbleau* grown in the region of Paris.

Planting   In November or December plant the young vines at 5 foot intervals along the wall and 1 foot in front of it.   Plant very firmly, stamping the soil as hard as you can.   Then cut down to a single cane with five buds.   Onto the wires behind each vine wire bamboo canes in a pattern which looks like this:

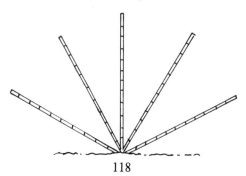

Year 1   Spring: the topmost bud of each vine will start to grow first, then the rest in order from the top downward.   This 'apical dominance' can be a nuisance.   If the lower shoots are badly inhibited by it, let the top shoot grow 3 feet and then pinch out its growing tip and any side shoots which appear until the other shoots are well away.

If you try to train very young, sappy vine shoots away from the way they want to go they will break off.   But as they grow, their base ripens and the ripeness spreads upwards.   In due course they will stand being bent about.   When this happens, begin training; and do it as follows: train the shoot from the topmost bud to an outside bamboo cane; the bending required will tend to offset its dominance.   Train the shoot from the next below to the other outside cane.   Train the shoot from the lowest bud to the middle cane; and the two middle ones to the two remaining canes.

In the first season not all the five canes will reach the top of the bamboos.   As soon as one does, stop it by pinching out the tip growth.   And throughout this and the next season pinch out the growing tips of all side shoots after 5 leaves have opened.

Year 2   Complete the process of building the structure of the vine.   If any flowers appear, pinch them off.   Allow side shoots to develop five leaves before pinching out their growing tips.   At the end of the season, when the leaves have fallen, you will have a five-branched fan of mature wood, the permanent structure; and on all of them a number of short side shoots.   Shorten these back to two buds each.

Year 3   Pinch out any growth which begins at the top of the 5 main 'ribs'.   The buds on the side shoots will grow into spurs and they will be bearing flower clusters.   Remove the flower clusters from the spur nearest the main rib, let it grow a foot long, pinch out its growing tip and as it develops sub side shoots, pinch out their growing tips when they have formed 2 or 3 leaves.   On the other spur remove all but one, the best, flower cluster and cut off the spur above the third leaf above the flower cluster.

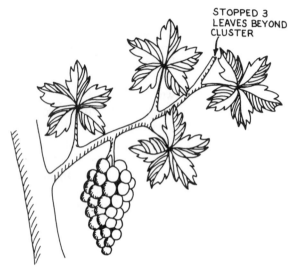

STOPPED 3
LEAVES BEYOND
CLUSTER

You will now have one bunch of grapes to each side shoot on each main 'rib'. At the end of the season, when it comes to the time to pick the grapes, *cut off the side shoot and the spur that has fruited as close to the first spur as you can*. The side shoot will then be carrying only the spur from which you removed the flowers. As soon as the leaves have fallen, cut that spur back to two buds—one to bear next year's fruit; and one to make the buds for the fruit of the year after next.

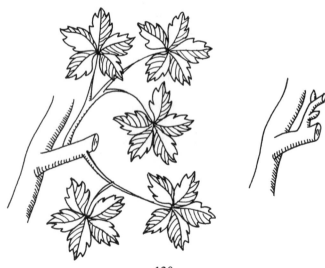

When pruning bear always in mind the one vital rule: *grapevines bear fruit only on wood of the previous season's growth.*

Grapes in unheated greenhouses *Varieties* Royal Muscadine (White), Alicante (Black), Black Hamburgh (Black, large), Madresfield Court (Black Muscat).

Grapevines in greenhouses are best grown as single cordons. You will need a narrow border of good garden soil along one outside wall of the house. Buy vines in pots, with a single cane at least 4 feet long and ripe all the way up, *ie* woody, not green and sappy.

At soil level, cut a hole in the wall of the greenhouse at least 3 inches in diameter, one every 24 inches. Opposite each hole, on the inside of the greenhouse, you will need to fix a taut galvanized iron wire from ground level, up the wall and then up to the ridge, on long galvanized iron vine eyes which hold the wire at least 10 inches from the wall and below the glass.

Plant one vine opposite each hole, in the outside border, thread the cane through the hole, tie it to the wire and cut it down to 4 buds above the hole. When the top shoot is growing in the spring and is sufficiently well-established to be safe, rub out the lower buds.

In all other respects, follow the instructions as for wall vines, above. In other words, crop and prune the cordons on the spur system. If, having regard to other plants which may be growing in the house, it is possible to keep doors and ventilators open in January, so as to expose the vines to frost, do so.

The outside bed should be mulched every year in spring with compost but I am against any richer manuring: it causes excessive growth which is very difficult to control.

Melons Three or four varieties of cantaloupe melons can easily be grown under cloches in Britain. Sow the seeds, one to a 3 inch pot, pressing them edgeways into the compost, in April. For germination and quick growth at the seedling state, they need a temperature of 68°F/70°F. Keep them warm, adequately watered, and expose to plenty of light.

Dig a trench one spit deep and wide along the row chosen for growing melons. Fill it with compost or stable manure, tread it down and flood it. As soon as the water subsides, replace the top soil in the form of a low ridge. Cover with cloches at

121

E

once, so as to warm up the soil.   A month's warming will not be too much.

Late in May, when the weather is warm, plant out the young melons at 3 feet intervals.   Keep the soil moist and, during the warm part of the day, open ventilators.   Keep the plants under observation and having chosen the two strongest shoots, pinch out the rest.   What you want is a shoot growing towards the next plant on the left and another towards the plant on the right.   When these main shoots overlap with those of the neighbours by six or seven inches, stop them by pinching out.   Meanwhile, side shoots will be developed and bearing flowers.   When the plants are in flower, give plenty of ventilation.   You need this to assist pollination.

The ideal to aim at is 4 fruits per plant.   But it is not easy to achieve.   Leaving pollination to chance you will average 2 fruits per plant.   One reason for this is that once a melon is 'set' and starts to grow from the fruitlet stage, it seems to draw all the strength of the plant into itself, and later ones never grow to a usable size.   Another problem which is hard to solve: suppose two or more fruits 'set' on the same day; the one nearest to the crown of the plant tends to grow at the expense of those further from the crown.

You may choose to try hand pollination.   I can tell you how to do it but cannot promise success.   First, you need to be able to recognize male from female flowers.   As it happens this is easy: the female flowers have a perfectly distinct miniature melon at the base; the males do not.   Next, you have to prevent chance pollination till you are ready to hand pollinate and the only way to do this is to pick off male flowers before they open, keeping one plant isolated, under a cloche or in the greenhouse, to ensure a supply when needed.

Keep the plants under observation.   As soon as you can see one female flower on each of four side shoots roughly equidistant from the crown of the plant, that plant is ready.   For success you need a sunny day.   Pick four male flowers which are fully open.   Holding a flower by the stem carefully tear off the petals to expose and isolate the central organs.   Thrust this central part, tip downwards, into the heart of an open female flower, and leave it there.   Do this to each of your four female flowers.

Stop the bearing side shoots by pinching out four leaves

beyond each fruitlet.   Stop all other side shoots after allowing three leaves to develop, by pinching out growing tips.

Melons are best if ripened on the plant.   As soon as the fruits begin to swell, carefully lift each one and slip under it a tile, a bit of slate, an inverted saucer, in other words anything to keep it clear of the soil, and fairly dry.   Continue watering until the fruits are about 4 inches in diameter (2½ inches in the case of Charentais) and then reduce watering to a minimum.   If the soil is moisture retentive, stop watering altogether as ripening approaches.

Melons are perfectly ripe for eating when a little crack begins to appear at the point where stalk and melon join.   A good guide to ripeness is your nose: the ripe melons give out the characteristic sweet, musky scent.

Varieties   At one time I had over a hundred varieties under cloches on trial—European, American and Russian.   Four which are reasonably reliable are Tiger; Dutch Net; Charentais; and Sweetheart.

Nectarines are smooth-skinned *peaches*.   See below.

Peaches   In Britain the best peaches are grown in hot houses: we can forget that, in these days of energy famine.   Under cool glass peaches are not easy to manage.   Excellent peaches can be grown on walls; but also, with care, in the open, as trees or bushes.   Trees or bushes, however, use up space in a way which is unsound practice in an 'intensive' garden.   Consequently I shall suggest a way of growing appropriate either for a wall, or on an espalier structure of the kind suggested for *apples* (see page 104).   So, either erect one or more such structures of posts and wires, or wire the face of the wall, which should face south, using vine-eyes hammered into the brickwork to hold the wires.

Varieties   The best peach for out of doors in Britain is Rivers' Peregrine ripening mid-August.   As peaches are 'self-fertile' you need not grow more than one variety but a good early peach is Early Rivers and a good late one is Late Rivers.   All are white fleshed, very superior to yellow peaches.   Nectarine Elruge is the best August variety and Rivers' Lord Napier excellent for September.   Where there is a choice, give your wall space to nectarines.

Preparation   Shaping peaches is no job for the amateur.   Buy fan-trained trees from the start. They cost twice as much as bush trees but save several years and probable failure. Spacing: four trees to our ten yard row. This will mean that the fans will ultimately overlap like this:

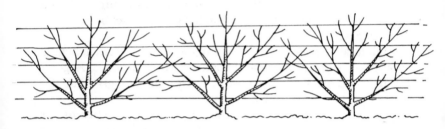

But it does not matter. Soil: prepare the rows by dressing with lime if there is likely to be a deficiency and with 2 ounces of coarse bonemeal per yard, hoed or rotovated in.

Planting Plant in November or December during a dry spell well above freezing. If you are not planting from containers, spread the roots carefully in the planting hole, and once they're covered with enough soil to protect them, heel and tread the soil very firmly indeed, and continue to do so until filling is complete. Tie the ribs of the fan to the wire. Stamp the soil really hard, then loosen the top inch with a hoe, and mulch with compost.

Management (including *Pruning*). The more pruning you do in spring and summer with your thumb-nail and the less in winter, the better.

(1) On the main ribs of your fans side shoots will grow and these will carry flowers and fruit.

(2) Sub-side shoots will grow on those side shoots. Let one about half-way up grow to five leaves, and stop it by pinching-out. Do the same to the one at the top of the shoot. Stop all the rest after only one leaf has developed. *One important exception:* allow the sub side shoot growing from the base of the side shoot, to grow to its full length—it will bear next year's peaches.

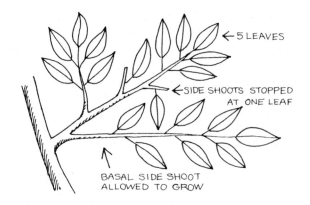

←5 LEAVES

←SIDE SHOOTS STOPPED
AT ONE LEAF

BASAL SIDE SHOOT
ALLOWED TO GROW

(3) Continue to pinch out unwanted side shoots. Your tree
has flowered. It has set fruit. The fruit has swelled to the
size of a cob nut. Go over it and remove as many as will leave
the remainder 3 inches away from each other.

(4) Continue to pinch out unwanted side shoots. The fruitlets have continued to swell. They are now the size of walnuts. Go over them again removing enough to leave the
remaining fruits 7 or 8 inches apart.

(5) Continue to pinch out unwanted side shoots. The most
delicious peaches are those which fall off as they ripen. The
patient and ingenious gardener devises a net into which the ripe
fruit can fall without bruising. Otherwise, visit the trees twice
a day, put the palm of your hand under the most advanced
fruits, and rock them. If the fruit falls into your hand, it's
ripe.

(6) All the fruit has been picked. Take your secateurs and
cut out every shoot which has borne fruit and tie the sub side
shoot to the wire in its place.

If the trees have been managed as suggested, no winter-
spraying should be necessary. Wait until spring and inspect
the trees thoroughly looking for dead wood; this is the result of
bacterial die-back. Cut back to healthy wood and paint over
the wounds with white lead paint.

Pests and diseases Aphids of several species may infest peach
trees. A winter wash with tar-oil (see *apples,* p. 110) will
reduce the incidence. If an infestation occurs spray with
'Malathion', or with a systemic insecticide such as 'Rogor'.

Die Back of the wood is caused by a bacterial infection. The

125

treatment recommended for Peach-leaf Curl will help to control it.

Peach-leaf Curl is a fungus disease of peach and almond trees and it *must* be prevented. The symptom is a gross deformity of the leaves which become thick and fleshy and curl into grotesque shapes, turning red, purple or yellow. Once it occurs you can do nothing except pick off and burn the leaves. But is can be prevented with success. Keep an eye on the trees in February and as soon as the flower-buds begin to swell, spray the trees very thoroughly—every twig and the ground between the trees as well—with Bordeaux Mixture, or a proprietary copper fungicide, or Lime Sulphur. As to the strength of the mixture, follow the maker's instructions. It may be as well to repeat the dose a week later in case you were too soon. The right moment may not come until March. This is usually an effective preventative of the only serious disease of peach trees.

Pears   For cultivation, pruning etc, and pest and disease control, see *apples* (pp. 103-111). This leaves only the subject of varieties.

Varieties   I do not consider that space should be wasted on early pears. They are all of indifferent quality. Second point: much better crops will be obtained if you plant two or more varieties which flower at the same time. Third point: grow only pears of the finest flavour and quality; they are no more trouble than those which are not so good. I suggest:

Williams, Bon Chretien to eat in September and to pollinate and be pollinated by

Packham's Triumph to eat in November.

Doyenne du Comice—by far the most delicious of all pears—to eat in November and December and pollinate and be pollinated by

Winter Nelis to eat in January and February.

I will name one variety whose quality is not up to those four, for two reasons: Conference sets by far the largest crop and never fails; and it is edible in October.

Plums   For preparation, planting etc, please see *peaches* (p. 123). The treatment is identical if, as I think you should, you buy fan-trained trees, *not* bushes. 'Victoria' plums do well on an east wall, or in the open, fan-trained on a wire structure and are easier in every way to manage like that.

126

For pruning see *cherries* (p. 113)—in other words do it all in spring and summer with your thumb-nail, by pinching out. If any cutting has to be done, do it in June. *Never cut a plum tree in winter.*

Varieties Keeping to the rule of growing only the best, I suggest that the prolific but indifferent varieties be eliminated and you grow for quality. But I should warn that it is not easy to grow plums to perfection in our climate. Next consideration: more than one variety, flowering at the same time, must be planted to ensure cross-pollination. But there is a difficulty: the very best, such as Coes's Golden Drop are very shy croppers excepting on a warm south wall or under glass and so, in my experience, are the delicious Reine Claude greengages. I suggest:

> Oulins Golden Gage to eat in mid August and to pollinate Comte d'Althan's Gage to eat mid September.
> Victoria (only very good when absolutely ripe) to be sure of crops (it is self-fertile), to eat in late August and to pollinate Early Rivers for eating in late July.

Damsons are better than other kinds of plums for cooking and for jam. Plant them as hedge-row trees or in any spare corners, let them look after themselves, and take what nature gives. They are ruggedly hardy, very beautiful in flower, extremely prolific and give very little if any trouble. Variety does not matter, but Cluster and Shropshire Prune are good.

Quince Not worth their space in an 'intensive' garden.

Raspberries, being native to Britain, are very easy to grow.
Preparation I am assuming that the soil where you are going to plant has received our routine cultivation and compost treatment. Mark out the rows 6 feet apart. For every 10 yard row you will need 15 raspberry canes. At each end of each row drive in a 3 x 3 oak post treated with copper preservative; and 2 x 2 posts at 10 feet intervals, between them. The posts should stand 5 feet tall after being driven in, so they should be 6½ feet long. Stretch 12 gauge galvanized iron wire taut between the end posts, and staple it to the intermediate posts; one wire at 2½ feet from the surface and one at 5 feet.
Planting Plant the canes in November, very firmly, treading in the soil as you fill the planting holes, at 2 feet intervals. Cut

down the canes to a bud at about 12 inches from the ground. During spring and summer a number of canes will grow from each root. Let them grow as tall as they like, tying them to the wire in a fan pattern.

Cultivation Keep down weeds by *shallow* hoeing: raspberry cane roots are very near the surface and are injured by deep cultivation. Mulch every spring with compost 2 inches deep.

Pruning In February cut all the canes of the ordinary summer-fruiting varieties down to 5½ feet tall. Cut autumn-fruiting varieties down to the ground. During the summer the cane which grew last year will bear fruit. Meanwhile, new cane will grow quite far from the rows. Pull or cut them out, but of the ones in or very near the row, retain the five strongest, tying them into the wire temporarily. Suppress the rest.

As soon as fruiting is over, cut out all the old canes, and burn them. This cutting should *not* be done so that stumps two or three inches long are left sticking up above the soil, but just *below* the surface. Now tie in the five canes of each crown in a fan pattern and leave them alone until next February.

Repeat this every year. A row of healthy raspberry plants regularly fed with compost by spring mulching, and kept clean of weeds and regularly pruned will last ten years. After that dig them up and start again with young canes in a different part of the garden.

Varieties Of the older varieties Lloyd George is the best. And of the new ones Malling Promise which is early, yielding a big crop of large berries. (There are some very new varieties with whose quality I am not familiar).

Autumn Fruiting: Lloyd George, if cut to the ground in February, gives a good autumn crop. The variety September is a good specifically autumn variety.

Pests and diseases Given good, clean cultivation and good drainage, none of the diseases of raspberries need worry you, with a single exception: the virus disease called Mosaic, the symptom of which is a mottling of the leaf in patches of light and dark green. There is no cure and it is important to dig up and burn diseased plants.

The same winter-wash with tar oil as you use on apple, pear and peach trees (see p. 110) will kill the eggs of aphids. Raspberry Beetle, whose grubs eat the fruit, can be a nuisance. Control by spraying or dusting with Derris, rather than a synthetic insecticide, 10 days after flowering begins and again 10 days after that.

Rhubarb is not, of course, a fruit but from the culinary point of view it is treated as if it were and so has a place here. You are very unlikely to want so much of it that you would plant a whole row; half-a-dozen roots should be quite enough for any ordinary household. The site chosen for it should be in full sun, away from the shade of trees and buildings.

Preparation Dig deep and manure the soil with compost or, if you can get it, stable manure or farmyard manure. Do this in winter. Plant the rhubarb 'crowns' in March or early April, in mild, dry weather. So that the crown itself is just above the soil surface. The interval between the crowns should be 3 feet.

Do not harvest any stalks in the first year. You may take a few from each plant in the second year and a full crop in the third and thereafter. Keep clear of weeds and mulch every winter with compost. *Warning* Although the stalks of rhubarb are, of course, wholesome, the leaves are poisonous.

Variety As most of us stop eating rhubarb as soon as real fruits begin to ripen in the garden, the only variety to plant is Timperley Early.

Pests and diseases None that need worry you.

Strawberries are of three kinds: the ordinary large summer-fruiting strawberries; the large autumn-fruiting or 'Perpetual' strawberries; and Alpine or *fraises des bois* strawberries. Alpine strawberries are dealt with separately at the end of this chapter.

Preparation Provided that the site chosen for your strawberry rows has been cultivated, composted and fertilized according to the suggested routine, no special preparation is necessary.

Planting The best planting time is August or September but you can plant until November. There is, however, a problem about early deliveries from nurseries; as you should buy only plants certified by the Ministry of Agriculture as free from virus disease, and as inspection prior to certification is done in September, August delivered plants will not have been certified. But reputable nurseries do not knowingly sell diseased plants.

Plant 15 inches apart in rows 30 inches apart. The crown of the plants should be at soil level and planting should be as firm as you can get it by pressing down the soil around the plant with your heel, thereafter loosening the top inch with a hoe, and mulching with compost. Keep the rows clear of weeds by hoeing. Irrigate freely in dry weather.

Varieties I suggest:

Early crop: Cambridge Vigour

Mid-season: Royal Sovereign—still the best English strawberry for flavour, but the crop is not so large.

Autumn crop: (August to November) Saint-Claude or Hampshire Maid.

Note Until this point treatment for both summer and autumn strawberries is the same. From this point onwards we must deal with them separately.

Summer Strawberries When, in the spring following planting the strawberry plants flower, pick off the flowers; for you should take no crop in the first year if you want to establish the plants really well.

As the plants grow they will produce runners—long growths with new young strawberry 'crowns'—two or three leaves and an embryo root system—along their length. If you need no more plants cut these off as close to the crown of the mother plant as you can or better still pinch them out when they are very small. If you need to increase stock, you can allow one runner, limited to one 'cadet' plant, per plant. To root the new plant, sink beside the mother plant a three inch pot full of compost, press the base of the 'cadet' plant into it, and secure it with a small wooden peg across the runner. As soon as the young plant is firmly rooted into the pot, cut it free of the mother plant and remove the pot to the nursery area for planting out in August.

Keep the rows weeded and watered.

In the second year you can take a crop. Again, remove all runners as soon as they show, or confine them to one, and to one 'cadet' per plant. In August take your shears and cut all the leaves off the plants close to the crown. Burn or compost them. New leaves, much healthier for the plants will begin to grow. Continue hoeing and removing the runners.

Owing to the incidence of virus disease (see below) you are unlikely to be able to keep your strawberry rows for more than 5 years and probably 4 years.   Hence the importance of a nursery of young stock taken from healthy mother-plants.

Strawing   Strawberries should be kept from contact with the soil.   You can buy mats to fit close round the plant; or you can tuck ordinary short barley or wheat straw tight round the plants for the fruit to rest on.   This should be removed to the compost bins at the same time as the old leaves.   There is an alternative method of getting rid of both straw and old leaves, feeding the soil with potash and killing disease organisms and pests all in one go: if the weather is dry, set fire to the straw at the windward end of the rows and let the fire run to the far end.   It will not hurt the crowns or roots.

Pests and diseases   I shall ignore those which though they *may* occur, usually do not.   Strawberries are attacked by aphids: they do not, as a rule, do much harm themselves, but unfortunately they are the vectors of a very serious virus disease.   There is no cure for this disease, but by killing the aphids you reduce the risk of your strawberry plants contracting the disease.   Keep very close watch on the undersides of the leaves by routine inspections and as soon as you see any sign of these greenfly, spray all your plants, especially the underside of the leaves, with a proprietary aphicide.   If you have to do this after the fruit has set, you will have to use an aphicide which is not toxic to people, *eg* Derris.

Birds are a serious pest of strawberries and raspberries.   The only effective protection is netting.   (See p. 134 on Fruit Cages).   Slugs are also a pest in strawberry beds.   They are easily controlled by putting down proprietary meta-fuel slug baits, but put them well away from the plants because while they infallibly kill the slugs, they also (it is why they are effective) attract them.

Autumn, or perpetual, Strawberries   Early in the nineteen-fifties I introduced into England 'remontant' or 'perpetual' strawberries from France, Germany and elsewhere.   In the late 19th century the French produced the first of these varieties, 'Saint Fiacre', and it was introduced here.   But whereas English breeders took no interest in it, the Continentals went on breeding these varieties and at one time I had scores of different ones under trial.   These strawberries are of several different habits: some produce 'flushes' of fruit from June until October (or November under cloches); others put out many runners

131

whose cadet plants root, flower and fruit at once, so that by the end of the season each mother plant is the centre of a square yard of fruitful offspring.

As a result of my experiments, reported in *Country Life* and in my book *Strawberry Growing Complete*, professional growers became interested and I can claim, without unbecoming want of modesty, to be responsible for the fact that home-grown autumn strawberries are now a commonplace in the markets. Those who are interested enough to go more thoroughly into this should read my *Strawberry Growing Complete* (Faber & Faber London, 1962). (Many of the varieties there named and described can be obtained only from French nurseries).

Plant and cultivate exactly as for summer strawberries, including the picking off of the flowers in May/June in the first year. But when they flower again later in the summer, you can leave the flowers and take a crop.

You will find that some perpetual strawberries make no runners. To increase stocks, lift the old plants and divide the sub crowns from the mother crown. Burn or compost the mother crown and replant the sub crowns.

Alpine Strawberries (*fraises des bois*) There are numerous varieties, some of which make runners while others do not. Those which do not are easier to control and can be used as edging plants, or as a catch crop between rows of fruit trees, raspberries, *etc*. The best of them is the variety, Baron Solemacher.

Raise the plants from seed sown under glass in trays of compost in March/April. Prick out either one to a pot into small pots as soon as they are big enough to handle, or into boxes at 4 inch intervals. Harden off in May/June and plant out, watering if the weather is dry, in July/August.

The plants fruit continuously throughout the summer and as they are perennials will last for three or four years after which they become awkwardly large and the size and quality of the fruit deteriorates, and you will need new plants raised from seed.

Space-saving ways of growing strawberries There are two: one is the well-known barrel method and is best explained in a drawing.

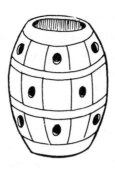

The diameter of the holes is 2 inches and they are about 12 inches apart in both directions—sideways and up and down. The way to plant is as follows. Cover the bottom of the barrel with drainage material—stones, shards etc. Then fill up to the first row of holes with a mixture of good top-soil or loam (50%), compost (35%) and coarse sand (15%), very thoroughly mixed and enriched with two or three handfuls of bonemeal to each barrow-load of soil.

Thread the roots of the plants in from the outside leaving the crown at the level of the hole, spread the roots. Now fill to the next row of holes. Make the soil very firm at each filling, by treading or pounding. Continue till the barrel is full. Plant half a dozen plants in the top. The only work thereafter will be pinching out runners and weeding the top. And, of course, watering to maintain soil moisture at, but not above, optimum level.

Such a strawberry barrel should give 3 years service before replanting becomes necessary. It should be stood in an open site. You will get a succession of fruit—south side first, then east, west and north.

The other method is based on the barrel method and is designed to save surface space by using vertical space. In front of the fence, wall or bank chosen for this job, drive 3 x 3 in wooden stakes into the ground at 3 foot intervals and 15 inches from the fence or bank. Onto these staple a sufficient length of small gauge, rigid plastic netting. Line it with black polythene. At one foot, two feet, three feet and four feet from the ground, cut 2 inch holes at 15 inch intervals.

Plant exactly as for the strawberry barrel, but you will have to do the firming of the soil more gently.

133

Birds and the fruitgrower

Most English gardeners like birds, so I shall lay myself open to protest when I say that the worst pests of the vegetable and fruit garden are birds. It is usually claimed that whereas vegetarian birds may be destructive of garden crops, carnivorous birds help the gardener by eating noxious insects, snails and slugs: this is true; and if the same birds eat large numbers of those most valuable of all animals to the farmer and gardener, earthworms, perhaps we can still spare them.

Vegetarian birds attack pea seedlings, lettuce and cabbage seedlings, and eat the buds and later the fruitlets of many fruit bushes and fruit trees. Often they peck off the buds—hundreds of them—without eating them and nobody seems quite sure why.

At all events, it may be well worth the serious food grower's while to put a part of his garden or allotment garden under netting; and to adapt his rotation plan so that, as well as the fruit trees and bushes, the most vulnerable vegetable and salad crops are grown under the net. If it were still a question, as it was in the past, of wire netting or heavy cotton fish net, I should hesitate to suggest this. But nylon and other plastic netting is light, easy to handle and relatively cheap. One or two firms of manufacturers specialise in fruit cages—aluminium uprights and cross members supporting the netting, and they are not ruinously dear. Gassons of Rye, Sussex, made the cage I use, but there are others. Or you can make the supporting structure yourself and buy the netting separately.

If you do not choose to do this, you will need a sufficient supply of pea guards—and peas are not the only crops you may need them for.

CHAPTER 8   THE ANNUAL CYCLE IN THE

600 SQUARE YARD PLOT

The first half of this double plot continues as described in Chapter 5.   The second half is basically a fruit garden but with a number of vegetable and salad catch crops (see the two alternative diagrams on the next two pages).   Although vegetables for the winter, that is brassica crops, can be planted out in the fruit garden, it is not, in my view, advisable; they are greedy feeders and they make winter tar oil spraying more troublesome since they have to be protected with polythene against the spray.   It is better to stick to short-term, ie catch crops or such crops as marrows, cucumbers and tomatoes which are cleared by November.

In diagram 1 the apples, pears, peaches, cherries and plums are to be trained on wire supports as *espalier* or fan trees, in the manner explained on pp. 104-9, so that space is left between rows for groundling crops.   Rows A and B are summer strawberries for the first three years; and rows C and D autumn-fruiting strawberries.   After three years these will be moved to rows E, F, G and H.   In the 7th and 9th year the strawberries can be shifted again to occupy J and O, after which they can be returned to A, B, C and D.

Red, white, and black currants are here grown as bushes, as are the gooseberries.   If the red and white currants, and the gooseberries were grown as 'cordons' there would be still more room for catch crops.   The dessert grapes are grown on the Guyot pruning and training method explained on p. 119, since they are being grown in the open and not on a wall.

In diagram 2 fruit trees are grown as bushes.   Easier, but less economical of space and not so convenient to work.

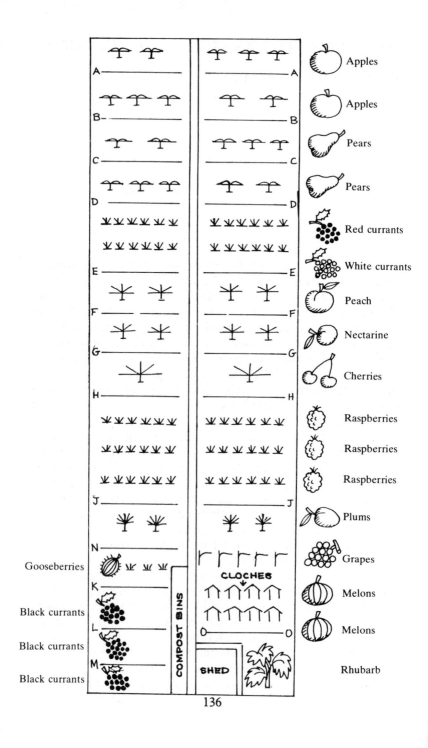

Apples

Apples

Pears

Pears

Red currants

White currants

Peach

Nectarine

Cherries

Raspberries

Raspberries

Raspberries

Plums

Grapes

Melons

Melons

Rhubarb

Gooseberries

Black currants

Black currants

Black currants

CLOCHES

COMPOST BINS

SHED

136

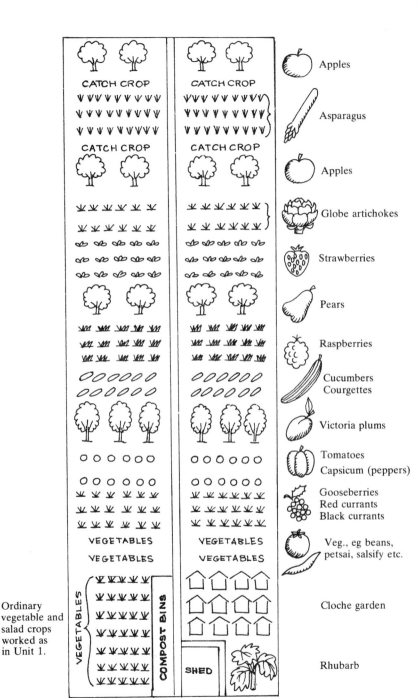

CATCH CROP

CATCH CROP

CATCH CROP

CATCH CROP

Ordinary
vegetable and
salad crops
worked as
in Unit 1.

VEGETABLES

VEGETABLES

VEGETABLES

VEGETABLES

VEGETABLES

VEGETABLES

COMPOST BINS

SHED

Apples

Asparagus

Apples

Globe artichokes

Strawberries

Pears

Raspberries

Cucumbers
Courgettes

Victoria plums

Tomatoes
Capsicum (peppers)

Gooseberries
Red currants
Black currants

Veg., eg beans,
petsai, salsify etc.

Cloche garden

Rhubarb

F

The working year

December

All fruit has been picked and catch crops harvested.

(1)   Spread compost over the entire area and rotovate thoroughly, hand hoeing between the plants where the rotovator will not go.

(2)   This garden will be run chiefly on the summer-pruning system and very little winter pruning need be done.   In fact the peaches, plums and cherries should not be pruned at all in winter.   But any pruning which the apples and pears may need at this season should be done now.   Prune the currants and gooseberries (pp. 115-117).

(3)   In the second half of December, thoroughly spray all the trees and bushes with tar oil (see p. 110), spray residues falling on the strawberries will not, at this season, do any harm.   Finally, rotovate again.

January

Cover rhubarb crowns with straw and inverted large pots, old buckets or boxes.   If a supply of fresh farmyard or stable manure is available, heap round these buckets; the heat of fermentation will force the rhubarb for an early supply.

February

(1)   Spread a general, balanced fertiliser at 1 oz. to the square yard and coarse bone meal at 1 oz. to the square yard, over the whole area, and rotovate.

(2)   Tip prune the raspberry canes (p. 128).

(3)   Prune and tie the grape vines (p. 119).

(4)   *Very important:* thoroughly spray the peach and nectarine trees with a copper lime or lime sulphur fungicide (p. 126).   If this essential spraying is followed by a rainy spell it may have to be repeated but it can be done only before flower buds begin to open.

March

(1)   As soon as growth starts, spray your strawberries with a mixture of 1 pint of lime sulphur and ½ oz. of nicotine in 10

gallons of water to control aphis, mildew and red spider mites.
(2)   Rotovate to suppress weeds as soon as growth begins.
(3)   Sow catch crops in E, F, G, H.   Suitable crops are lettuce, radish, turnips and carrots for eating young.   Sow
spinach for harvesting in May in the other catch crop pos-
itions.   Alternatively, longer-term crops, *eg* marrows and
cucumbers may be planted but choose bush varieties, not trailing varieties.
(4)   At the flowerbud-burst stage of your pear trees—end of
March—spray the trees thoroughly with lime sulphur (2½ pints
per 10 gallons of water) to control scab.
(5)   Sow tomato seeds in heat under glass.

April   NB   When spraying fruit trees, catch crops between the
rows must be covered with a sheet of polythene.

(1)   At the green flower stage of the pear blossom and bud-
burst stage of the apple blossom (mid April) spray apples and
pears with lime sulphur to control scab (2½ pints per 10 gallons
water).   At the end of the month—'white-bud' stage—spray
again but use only ½ pint of lime sulphur to 10 gallons of water.
(2)   When black currant flowers are visible as a tight,
unopened cluster, spray with lime sulphur—1½ pints to 10
gallons of water, to control Big Bud Mite.
(3)   Late in April gooseberries will be 'setting' fruit.   A dusting with sulphur will prevent American Mildew but this is not a
very important control and can be omitted.
(4)   Sow melon seeds under glass and in heat early this month
and begin to harden off the seedlings by lower temperatures
towards the end of the month.
(5)   Prune peach, nectarine, plum and cherry trees if pruning
is necessary (see Fruit Dictionary).
(6)   Rotovate as necessary.

May

(1)   At apple-blossom pink-bud stage, spray the trees with
lime sulphur at ½ pint to 10 gallons water.   Same treatment for
the pears at petal-fall stage and again for the apples—later—at
petal-fall stage.
(2)   About May 15 spray plum trees with Derris—3 ozs. to 10

gallons of water—to control sawfly and winter moth cater-pillars. A similar spray applied to gooseberries controls sawfly on them. A dusting with Derris dust late this month controls Raspberry Beetle by killing the larvae.

(3) Just before the strawberry flowers open in mid May, repeat the lime sulphur spray given in March.

(4) Late in the month plant out melons under the cloches.

(5) From now onwards you must begin to watch all the fruit trees and carry out the routine pruning by pinching out: see Fruit Dictionary.

(6) Clear remainder of spinach crop and plant out tomatoes in cleared rows.

(7) Re-sow catch crops as necessary. Maintain rotova-tion. Irrigation may become necessary.

June

(1) In mid June spray cherry trees with Derris at 3 ozs. to 10 gallons of water, to control Cherry Sawfly.

(2) Same treatment on gooseberries at the end of the month to control the second brood of sawfly.

(3) Continue pinching out as necessary.

(4) Pinching out of melons (p. 122) begins.

(5) Tie tomatoes and pinch out side shoots (p. 98).

(6) Rotovation and irrigation as required. Successional sow-ings of catch crops.

July

(1) If there is a history of Leaf-Spot Fungus on black currants in your neighbourhood, a spray with copper lime fungicide in late July helps to control it.

(2) Repeat the lime sulphur spray on strawberries *after* the fruit has all been harvested.

(3) Grapes will require attention. Tie the fruiting shoots to the higher wire and stop them. Tie in the replacement canes and do necessary pinching out.

(4) Tomatoes and melons will both require routine attention.

(5) Successional sowings of catch crops.

(6) Rotovation as required. Irrigation, if necessary. Cherr-ies will be harvested. Last summer strawberries will be har-vested. Raspberries will be harvested; and other soft fruit.

August

Routine tasks only: pinching out on trees, vines, melons and tomatoes; rotovation to suppress weeds; irrigation may be necessary although August often has adequate rainfall. You will be harvesting peaches, nectarines and plums. Successional sowings of catch crops may be required.

September

Routine tasks as in August. You will harvest some tomatoes and the first melons; and early apples and pears if you have planted early varieties. And, of course, autumn strawberries.

October

Routine tasks as in August and September—but by now there should not be much pinching out to be done and while rotovation must be maintained, there will be no need for any irrigation. You will be harvesting apples, pears, grapes, melons and tomatoes, and the last of the autumn strawberries. (Those which ripen in November are virtually tasteless.)

November

You should harvest the last of the pears; finish off the catch crops, clear the whole area of rubbish, and begin to spread compost from the bins.

Pests

Birds of several species are the worst pest of fruit gardens. I have already referred to this in the last Chapter and elsewhere. Bull-finches, tits and others pick off the buds; pigeons and others eat fruitlets—I have found over 300 in the crop of a pigeon—blackbirds and thrushes eat strawberries, cherries and raspberries. A number of birds ruin ripening peaches, pears, apples and plums by picking holes in them. No bird-scaring devices are effective for more than a few hours, not even kites simulating hawks.

The only protection is nylon netting. One of the advantages of growing fruit, as espalier and fan-trained trees rather than standards is that they are much easier to net.

The ideal solution is to cover the whole fruit garden by putting it into a netting cage. A cage 6 feet tall and big enough to cover 300 square yards, with aluminium uprights and cross-members and nylon netting, would, however, cost at least £170.

Wasps are a nuisance in fruit gardens, although from my own observation, I should say that they can only attack fruits which have already been damaged by birds. The most radical control is to seek and destroy the wasps' nests. Finding them requires great patience and keen eyesight, for it entails watching wasps in flight and following them. Nests are usually made in holes in banks, hollow trees or some such shelter. Cyanide is the most effective killer but it is dangerous stuff to have and to handle. Nests in banks can be dealt with by marking them in daylight and returning after dark with a can of paraffin and a funnel. Pour paraffin into the entrance hole and put a match to it. There are some proprietary wasp killers on the market.

How much time will it cost you?

Time consumed by work in the fruit garden is considerable. I shrink from trying to estimate it and can give you only the roughest idea. It should not take you more than 30 minutes to rotovate the whole plot: from March to October you may have to do it once a week to keep the garden in perfect order. So, 2 hours a month from March to October, an hour a month in November and December, none in January and February.

Spraying thoroughly takes time: allow 30 minutes for assembling the gear and mixing the spray, 30 minutes to spray a ten yard row of espalier and fan-trained trees really carefully, and 20 minutes for remixing. You will have to allow at least ten hours for this in December, but then none until March; then, say, an average of five hours a month until July.

Summer pruning with your thumb-nail—June to September—will demand between 2 and 4 hours a week—less time as you get the hang of it. Then there's the work on the catch crops.

On the whole and by sticking strictly to routines and not letting the garden get away from you, I would guess that you should not need to give this garden more than 5 hours a week. So, if you are already managing the Unit Plot, you can easily manage Unit x 2 if you have retired but, if you are still in 'gainful' work, you may need the help of another member of your household, or of a part-time gardener, *eg* an OAP who wants to earn a little extra money.

Returns and costs

To answer this I have to assume that you make a success of the garden. You should get 50 lbs of apples and 50 lbs of pears; between 30 and 40 lbs of red and white currants; between 30 and 50 peaches or nectarines from each tree; as many strawberries as you can eat (family of four), and a surplus of raspberries; enough gooseberries and currants to make about 75 lbs of jam or jelly; between 20 to 30 melons. The 5 'Royal Muscadine' grape vines will yield between 25 and 50 bunches of grapes, the largest of which will weigh about 8 ozs. Cherries? God knows. Plums? Either so many you won't know what to do with them, or none—it depends on the weather in March and April. To this harvest you must add the catch crops which I have no means of estimating.

In short, the value you get for your investment in stock (£150), in a rotovator which, however, will sharply reduce your labour time in Unit 1, pesticides, fertiliser, water and rent-equivalent, will be something like £150 worth of fruit and salads, possibly £200 worth—but *plus* a number of such unquantifiable benefits as pleasure, profitable (instead of expensive) exercise and recreation, and social usefulness.

PART 3   THE PLOT x 4 — OR QUARTER OF AN ACRE PLOT

CHAPTER 9   LAYOUT OF THE PLOT x 4

There are innumerable combinations of fruit and vegetables which can be fitted into a garden of the same size.   How about trying a combination of vegetables, fruit, wine and tobacco? It may serve somebody's purpose to see how, in terms of time and money, it works out.   What I have in mind is a garden to be worked either single handed by a man or woman willing and able to give the garden between 3 or 4 hours a day; or, if that's not possible, to employ casual labour to help with some of the tasks.   The object is to keep a household of half a dozen people in vegetables, fruit and tobacco and a little wine.

How much land is needed?   We have already seen that you can get enough vegetables for an average household off one unit of 300 square yards (10 rods), provided you do the job well.   And that by using the inter-rows in the fruit garden (Unit x 2) the quantity of vegetable and salad crops can be substantially increased.   But no provision has been made for wine and tobacco and while the fruit garden will yield enough soft fruit (including a surplus of raspberries to go into the deep freeze—see Appendix—if you have one) and some other crops, we could do with more tree fruit.   So to the basic 600 square yards—two Units—we need to add more land.

The smallest vineyard you require in order to provide a significant amount of wine, say 5 bottles a week throughout the year, will be enough to accommodate 300 grape vines.   That is 300 square yards.   That brings us to Unit x 3, and the total size of the subsistence garden is now 900 square yards.   And we still have the tobacco and extra fruit to accommodate.   A quarter of an acre is more than 1,200 square yards (Unit x 4).   Let's see what can be done with quarter of an acre.

Design imperatives

(a)   A layout which makes it possible to rotovate through straight rows with a minimum of impediment.

(b)   An irrigation system which reaches every part of the garden with a minimum of hose movement.

(c)   A system of paths giving easy access to the whole area.

(d)   Grouping of crops so that those most vulnerable to birds are protected.

(e)   Grouping of fruits such that pest control spraying is made easy.

In other words, at this size level the garden should be designed with far more regard to the commodity on which it makes the heaviest demand—labour.

Notes on the diagram

(1)   The apples and pears are grown as espaliers—see pp. 104-9—in continuous long rows to facilitate rotovating, compost spreading and pest control spraying.

(2)   The vineyard is planted on the same principle—long, continuous rows eliminate a lot of manoeuvring of the cultivating and spraying machinery.

(3)   The rows numbered 1 to 41 are vegetables and salads.   They are to be worked on the same continuous cycle plan as that described in Chapter 5.

(4)   The area BCDE is under a permanent cage of nylon netting to protect the crops against birds.   It is suggested, therefore, that the vegetable rows 1 to 9 be used for the most vulnerable of these crops, *eg* peas and lettuces.

(5)   The compost bins should be on that side of the path which is nearest to the south, so that the back of the bins, which can be of timber, faces as nearly south as possible.   The back, whitewashed, can then be used by training two fan-trained nectarine trees to it.   They are big enough to enable you to produce enough compost to cover the whole garden 1 inch deep once per annum.

(6)   The plums and peaches are fan-trained.   See pp. 123 and 126.

(7)   The tobacco plot will carry fifty plants which should yield as much dried leaf as you are allowed free of duty.

ENCIRCLED NUMBERS REFER YOU TO THE NOTES

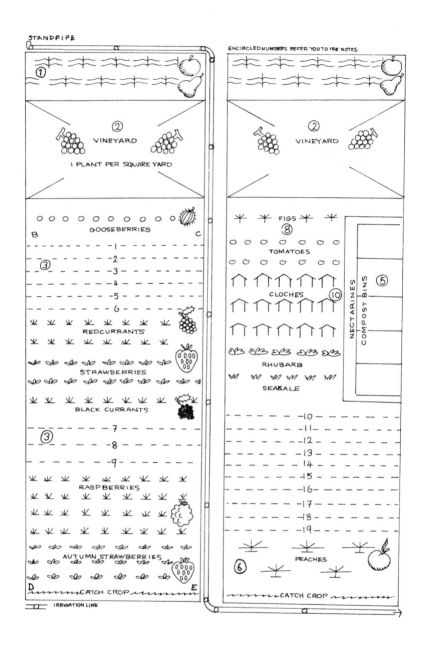

①

② VINEYARD
1 PLANT PER SQUARE YARD

② VINEYARD

○ ○ ○ ○ ○ ○ ○ ○ ○ ○
GOOSEBERRIES

B   C
— — — — — —1— — — — — —
③ — — — — —2— — — — — —
— — — — — —3— — — — — —
— — — — — —4— — — — — —
— — — — — —5— — — — — —
— — — — — 6 — — — —

REDCURRANTS

STRAWBERRIES

BLACK CURRANTS

— — — — —7— — — — — —
③ — — — —8— — — — — —
— — — — —9— — — — — —

RASPBERRIES

AUTUMN STRAWBERRIES

D ⁓⁓⁓⁓⁓CATCH CROP⁓⁓⁓⁓⁓ E

⊏▭⊐ IRRIGATION LINE

✳ ✳ FIGS ✳ ✳
⑧
○ ○ ○ ○ ○ ○ ○ ○
TOMATOES
○ ○ ○ ○ ○ ○ ○

CLOCHES ⑩

RHUBARB

SEAKALE

— — — — —10— — — —
— — — — —11— — — —
— — — — —12— — — —
— — — — —13— — — —
— — — — —14— — — —
— — — — —15— — — —
— — — — —16— — — —
— — — — —17— — — —
— — — — —18— — — —
— — — — —19— — — —

PEACHES
⑥

⁓⁓⁓⁓⁓CATCH CROP⁓⁓⁓⁓⁓

NECTARINES   ⑤
COMPOST BINS

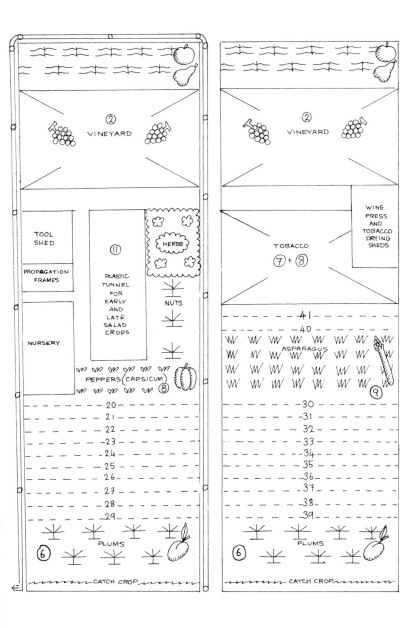

(8)   The three crop plants belonging to the family *Solanaceae* are placed as far apart as possible—tomatoes, peppers and tobacco; all are capable of conveying the virus disease, Mosaic to the others.   The pepper variety Canape (Thompson & Morgan) is the only one which will ripen its fruit in the open.

(9)   You may wish to sell some crops.   Asparagus fetches a high price; hence the considerable space allotted to it.

(10/11)   The plastic tunnel is the cheapest solution to the greenhouse problem.   It will accommodate lettuce, tomatoes, peppers, aubergines and cucumbers.   Also, if you wish, melons.   See Appendix iii for details of glass and plastic.

CHAPTER 10   THE VINEYARD

The history of wine growing in England begins in the third century AD when the Roman Emperor Probus repealed (280 AD) a law of the Emperor Domitian which was designed—but in much of the Empire failed—to prevent the planting of vineyards outside Italy.   For a thousand years vineyard cultivation in England increased very slowly, and more or less wine of varying quality was produced   In the mid fourteenth century viticulture began to decline, chiefly for economic reasons, but there is no century between the third and our own in which there has not been at least one vineyard somewhere in Britain.

The Marquis of Bute's large vineyard in Glamorganshire having been grubbed up in 1920, there was then no vineyard in Britain until 1948 when R. Barrington Brock planted his experimental one at Oxted in Surrey and I planted mine at Shottenden in Kent.   Both of us introduced from the Continent those very early fruiting, early ripening varieties of the wine vine which seemed most likely to succeed in our climate.   And both of us, R. Barrington Brock much more systematically and scientifically endowed than me, experimented with the numerous ways of pruning vines to find that which gave the best result in this country.

As a result of our work, and following the publication in books and articles of our results, there are now numerous small and a few larger vineyards in England and Wales; a few of these are commercial and there are now several English-grown wines of very fair quality on the markets, in small quantities.   The doyen of these English commercial wine growers is General Sir Guy Salisbury-Jones whose 'Hambleden' white wine is the best of the English wine and is on the wine list of one or two Paris restaurants. I should add here that I am not concerned in this chapter with making wine by using kits bought at the chemists, nor with the making of wine with fruits or vegetables, *ie* what are called 'country wines'. Some of these can be good and if that is what you want to make then the best book I know on the subject is *Country Wines* by H. M. Aylett. But here I am concerned to tell you how to grow wine grapes, nothing more.

Phylloxera vastatrix

Here, to start with, is a piece of history which every prospective grower of wine-grapes should know, partly because it may affect his choice of varieties, and in any case because it has a bearing on the method of cultivation. For thousands of years the numerous varieties (several thousand) of the wine vine (*Vitis vinifera*) were grown in the Old World on their own roots, being propagated by cuttings and layering. In the second half of the last century grape vines of the same genus (*Vitis*) but of other species, from North America, were introduced into Europe. With them, unnoticed, came an aphis of the genus *Phylloxera*, and later named *vastatrix* (the devastator). Because the American vines had, for hundreds of thousands of years evolved with and at the same time as this parasite on the genus *Vitis*, they had developed a high degree of tolerance and grew perfectly well in spite of its presence, just as animals are tolerant of fleas parasitic on them. But since this aphis was not native to any part of Europe or Asia or Africa, the Old World vines had evolved no such tolerance. Consequently, when the aphis began to colonise the European vineyards, the result was devastating: millions of vines were killed, the French, Italian and Spanish wine industry, was nearly wiped out, and the losses to France alone were greater than those—financially—of the Franco-Prussian War.

Phylloxera vastatrix attacks the roots of Old World vines. The problem posed by its devastation was eventually solved by grafting the old European varieties onto American vine roots. Today the vines of all the great vineyard regions, are grafted onto American stocks. This is perfectly satisfactory in all but one respect: we have not exterminated *P. vastatrix*; we have learned to live with it, a fact which is particularly significant for English viticulture.

152

Although the aphis was first seen and examined in Europe in the greenhouse variety of a commercial grape-grower in Ramsgate, the creature never established itself here, chiefly because there was, at the time, only one vineyard in Britain, and that in Glamorganshire, remote from the focus of infection.   Consequently, when Brock and I started our experiment, we were able to grow our vines, from cuttings, on their own roots.   Both of us published appeals to those growers and gardeners who might follow our example, to import no rooted vines, but only cuttings, from the Continent or from America. These appeals went unheeded, and it is now, in my opinion, certain that *Phylloxera* is busy establishing itself here.   It is true that all plants imported into Britain have to have a phytosanitary certificate certifying them free from disease, and pests; but I have witnessed the casual ease with which such certificates are issued in France and Italy.

It would, therefore, now be foolish to plant vineyards of vines on their own roots and grafting onto resistant stocks will have to be regarded as necessary here as it is elsewhere in Europe.   I could, of course, be wrong about this: but it is only fair to warn you.

What yield can you expect?

An old grapevine correctly pruned on a south wall, produces hundreds of bunches of grapes and can fill *scores* of bottles of wine from a single root.   The great 'Black Hamburgh' vine in the Hampton Court vinery produces about 3000 bunches of grapes per year.

But we are not here concerned with vines on walls and under glass.   The way in which wine vines are cultivated has to be governed by soil, by climate and by the quality of the wine you want to make.It is not for nothing that the French and Germans keep the vines of the great vineyard regions very small, very closely planted, and very near the soil surface.   The first great scientific agronomist, Mago of Carthage, discovered the connection between severe restriction of the vine and quality of wine and his findings were adopted and adapted for European conditions by the Romano-Spanish agronomist Columnella in the 3rd century BC.   Numerous French, Italian, Spanish and German experts have confirmed those early results.

I am making a point of this because some of the new English viticulturists are being influenced by American and Australian practice, the practice of planting fewer vines to a given area, training them longer and much higher, and taking from each a much larger crop. It may be that these methods are suitable for hotter and dryer climates than ours, though neither country has yet produced by those means wines equal to the best of Europe's, whereas wines which were of superlative quality were produced, in the past, from the Lilyvale Deering Vineyards (Australia) and the Napa Valley (California).

If the planting density, training and pruning methods, which I suggest below, based upon the best French and German practice, be adopted, the amateur may expect a vintage at the rate of about 3000 bottles of wine per annum per acre. He may do better; quite possibly he may not do nearly as well. He will not attain that figure until the vineyard's sixth year. the divergence between yields from place to place, from variety to variety and from site to site, is very wide: in the northernmost European vineyards it may be as low as 80 hectolitres per hectare, (about 3200 quarts per acre); in the south European vineyards yields as high as 250 hectolitres per hectare are common. In my view an English vineyard which yields at the rate of 2000 bottles per acre justifies itself. Not, of course, that we need think in terms of acres.

Preparation

I assume that the soil chosen for your vines has been cultivated and composted in the way suggested elsewhere in this book. A single vine trained and pruned in the manner described below will occupy a space of 1 square yard, so a row of 100 vines would be 100 yards long and one yard wide; the same 100 vines will go into a 10 yard x 10 yard square. An acre will hold 4,840 vines. Think of the yield in wine as being at about half a bottle per square yard. I had better repeat that by other training and pruning methods you can get more: more and worse. In my Kent vineyard I got my yield, by the method described below and with the varieties I advocate, up to one bottle per square yard.

To support a row of vines you need, at each end of the row, a very stout post—6 x 6 in is not excessive—driven so far into the ground that it is really firm and stands three feet above the ground.

If the rows are to be longer than 10 yards, then you will need 3 x 3 in posts at 10 yard intervals between the two big ones.

If there is more than one row, then set the rows one yard apart.

At 15 inches and 30 inches respectively from the soil surface stretch taut galvanised iron wire. If the row is more than 10 yards long, and there are therefore intermediate posts, staple these two wires to them.

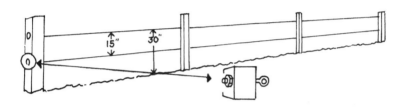

Dig or rotovate the soil which will have been trodden down during this operation and keep it clean until you are ready to plant.

Varieties

No dessert variety of grape vine is really suitable for making wine excepting Royal Muscadine (or *Chasselas Doré*). Red wines are produced by fermenting black grapes with their skins in which alone the red pigment is concentrated. White wines are produced by fermenting either white or black grapes without the skins. It has hitherto proved impossible to produce in our climate, a red wine fit to drink. We are confined to white wine. The reasons are known but need not detain us here.

In the course of experimental work referred to at the beginning of this chapter, more than a hundred vine varieties from all over Europe and America were tried, and about a dozen selected as promising in our climate. If I name all of them, not to mention others which have been tried since then by other growers, it will face the reader with a choice he can make only by guessing. I shall therefore name only three varieties, two of them for everyone, the third for growers in favoured regions. Other men experienced in vine growing will have their own different ideas; I have not tested them so cannot offer an opinion.

(1) *Riesling-Sylvaner* which is probably the same, or as nearly so as to make no difference as *Müller-Thurgau*. It is probably a hybrid between two very famous varieties grown in the Rhine and Moselle vineyards. It is, therefore, a pure *Vitis vinifera* (Old World wine vine) cultivar and as such susceptible to the American vine pests and diseases (see below), to which, however, in my experience, it shows remarkable resistance. It is a stout, vigorous plant producing medium-sized bunches of medium-sized grapes in great number, grapes which yield a white wine of good quality.

(2) *Seyve-Villard* 5.276. When *Phylloxera* nearly wiped out the Old World vines, as described above, French nurserymen began trying to cross breed Old World and New World grapes to produce a hybrid with the fine flavour of the Old World wine grapes and resistance to *Phylloxera* and to two American fungus diseases of the vine (see below). For reasons I shall not go into here, these hybrid vines, some of which yield excellent wines, are frowned on by the French authorities, but that need not worry us. This variety is one of the best of the early-maturing hybrids. Partially resistant to *Phylloxera* it is, in my experience, very resistant to the two worst fungus diseases. It is a heavy cropper, producing relatively large and beautifully shapely bunches of golden grapes of medium size. It is not as vigorous as *Riesling-Sylvaner* but quite vigorous enough.

(3) *Pinot Meunière* or Miller's Burgundy. The history of this vine is remarkable. A miller (or his wife—*meunière*) is, of course, dusted white with flour. The leaves of this vine are a silvery grey-green because covered with a fine, white tomentum. As a consequence it is very easy to distinguish even in a description, which enables me to say that it was one of the varieties described by Pliny as cultivated by the Romans, who may well have introduced it here. On the other hand like its close relative, *Pinot Noir*, it is much grown in Burgundy. *Pinot Noir* is one of the *cépages nobles*—noble wine vines—and is widely planted in Champagne. A famous Champagne grower who keeps a kindly eye on the Hambledon vineyard which, on my advice, was originally planted half with *Riesling-Sylvaner*,

156

and the other half with S.V. 5.276, suggested adding *un peu de noblesse* to the wine, and as a result some *Pinot Noir* has been planted there.   I believe that *Pinot Meunière* would do as well and it is decidedly earlier and therefore more suitable in our climate.   I suggest, however, that it should only be risked by those planting a vineyard in the 10 mile coastal strip of England from Lowestoft in the north east to Cornwall in the south west.   It is a question of getting enough sunshine to ripen this superlative wine grape.

Miller's Burgundy, is, of course, a pure *vinifera* and so susceptible to the American pests and diseases of the vine.

Where to buy wine grape vines:

It is not my business to tell you where to buy vineyard vines, but since you may have difficulty in finding a source of supply, I will make some suggestions.   Two very well-known nurseries carry stocks of some varieties: Messrs Jackman and Co. of Woking, Surrey; and Messrs Thomas Rivers and Co. of Sawbridgeworth, Herts.   Messrs B. T. Ambrose, Nether Hall, Cavendish, Sudbury, Suffolk offer supplies of grafted vines. Gillian Pearkes, of Rhyll Manor, Dulverton, Somerset, offers not only a range of suitable varieties, but also a book, *Growing Grapes in Britain*.   Messrs J. G. & I. M. Barrett, The Vineyards, Cricks Green, Felsted, Essex offer grafted vines imported from France and Germany, and also many varieties on their own roots and cuttings for rooting by the purchaser.   Bernard Theobald of Westbury Farm, Purley, Reading, Berks offers one-year-old vines on their own roots.

Planting

Plant in November/December during mild, dry weather at intervals of 3 feet in rows 3 feet apart.   Dig the planting holes big enough to enable you to spread the roots, and if you are planting grafted vines, keep the graft junction, which will be obvious, *above* the soil surface. Fill in carefully and very firmly by treading and heeling thoroughly.   Young vines correctly raised will have only a single cane: shorten each to six or seven buds.

NOTE: Any piece of living vine wood of the last season's

growth, between a quarter and half an inch in girth and from nine inches to a foot long, if planted to three quarters of its length, will begin to grow in spring and soon form roots.

During the winter stick a 6 foot bamboo cane into the soil by each vine and tie or wire it to each of the galvanised iron wires. In early March, prune the vines by cutting down to only three buds, so that you are left with nothing but short stumps. The buds will begin to grow in May. As soon as they are safely away and growing well, reduce their number to two—the strongest two—on each one by breaking off the weakest of the three.

During the growing season keep both shoots lightly tied to the bamboo cane, and pinch out the tips of the side shoots after one leaf has developed. Keep the vineyard clear of weeds by hoeing. When the shoots reach the top of the bamboo cane, stop them by pinching out.

Routine disease control

Powdery Mildew (*Uncinula necator*) is one of the fungus diseases of the vine introduced accidentally from America and now established here. It is sometimes referred to as *Oidium*.

It is unlikely to put in an appearance before July. It manifests itself as a very fine, light-coloured, dusty film on leaves, green stems and fruits, but usually starts on the surface of leaves. The S.V. 5.276 vines are very resistant to this desease, but the other two recommended varieties are not.

Beginning in late June spray the vines with lime sulphur at a strength of 1 part of lime sulphur to 150 parts of water, at intervals of 3 weeks until the grapes begin to ripen, after which there is no further danger. Do the spraying either when the weather is overcast or late in the evening; if done in full sunshine it causes spray burn.

Downy Mildew (*Plasmopara viticola*) is the second fungus disease introduced from America. In England its incidence is higher and the damage it does is more serious than Powdery Mildew. It first manifests itself as what looks like an oily, transparent patch on the upper surface of the leaf; it also appears on young stems and on the fruitlets. The corresponding area on the underside of the leaf becomes covered with dense, white down.

This fungus is what is called 'endophytic'—*ie* its mycelium grows not on the surface of the leaves like powdery mildew, but inside the leaf tissue.   Consequently, once established, it is incurable by spraying.   But there is a stage in its life cycle when it is extremely vulnerable to destruction by minute quantities of copper; this is the stage when its free-swimming zoospores are swimming about in drops of water on the leaves, seeking a breathing pore into which to insert a 'germ tube'.

Control is by prevention.   As soon as the vines have opened about half of their buds into leaves, spray with a copper lime fungicide.   Both sides of the leaves and all parts of the vines must be well covered.   If the weather is wet, repeat this treatment once a fortnight until ripening begins, then stop.   If dry, then once every three weeks will be sufficient.   Three sprayings are vital; the first, following burgeoning; the second, just before flowers open; and just after the grapes have set.

In general, the aim should be to keep the vines covered with copper residues throughout the growing season.

There are other diseases of the vine and, as well as *Phylloxera*, a few insect pests.   But their incidence is, in my experience, so low that it is usually safe to forget about them.   A full account of all the diseases and pests of the vine will be found in *Vineyards in England* (ed Edward Hyams, Faber and Faber London, 1954) which is out of print but can be borrowed from libraries.

One pest of vineyards, by far the most destructive, must be mentioned: birds.   They will eat your whole crop unless you cover the vineyard with netting.

Pruning and cropping

At the end of the first season each of your vines will consist of two 6 foot long canes growing from a short stumpy trunk.   In England it is usually safe to prune anytime in the winter and up to mid March.   Some will be stout and strong—the canes up to half an inch in girth.   Others will be weaker, some much less than 6 feet tall, and very thin.

Deal first with these weaker vines.   Cut out the weaker of the two canes at its junction with the trunk; cut the other back to 3 buds. Now the stronger vines. Remove all ties.   Choose the stronger and stouter of the pair of canes, tie it loosely to the bamboo just below the level of the bottom wire;

bend it gently down and tie it at two points to the lower wire. It will then overlap the next vine in the row. Cut it off below a bud level with the next vine (so that the bud is removed). Then cut down the other cane to 3 buds.

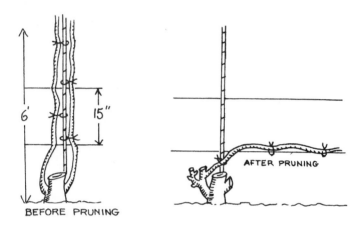

BEFORE PRUNING

AFTER PRUNING

In the second season the following growth will occur.

(1) From the 3-bud stump, three shoots. As soon as they are growing well away, reduce to two by breaking off the weakest. Keep the other two tied to the bamboo as they grow, pinch out side shoots after one leaf has developed, and stop at six feet by pinching out.

(2) From each of the buds on the cane tied to the lower wire will spring a shoot, beginning at the one furthest from the root. Each of these shoots will have formed one to three flower clusters opening at about the same time as the wild elderberry flowers—late June or early July. When these shoots have grown tall enough to be tied easily to the upper wire, stop them by pinching out the growing tip and tie them to the wire. (See diagram on p. 162).

(3) Side shoots may try to grow from these fruiting shoots. Allow one leaf to develop and then pinch them out.

(4) As soon as grapes have set they will at first grow quite fast. But then will come a pause when for some time they seem to grow no larger. Don't worry: they are making their pips. As soon as that has been done, they begin to swell again.

A day comes in late September or early October when the grapes begin to look less hard and green; they acquire a look of translucence, almost as if they might become transparent. They are beginning to ripen.

When are wine grapes ripe enough?

The answer, in England, is, in one word, never.   In the making of English wine the process of *chaptalisation* (the adding of a suitable and, under EEC rules, legally permissible, kind of sugar to the *must*—the grapes in the press or the first fermentation vat) is necessary in 9 years out of 10, as it is in the Rhine and Moselle vineyards.

Here, briefly, is the reason: in the process of fermentation grape sugar is turned into alcohol by yeasts: 1 per cent of sugar yields 0.5 degrees of alcohol in the wine.   A wine which has less than 8 degrees of alcohol is worthless; it should have at least 9 and preferably 10 or 11.   Let us take 9 as the lowest figure to aim for.   If we are to get 9 degrees of alcohol, the grapes must contain 18 per cent sugar in their juice.   Now, here is the catch: by numerous experiments Ray Barrington Brock found that grapes with a sugar content of 12 per cent taste sweet to many people, and at 13 per cent we all find them sweet.   But at 13 per cent they would yield a wine of only 6.5 degrees—miserable stuff.   Moreover, it would be unpalatable because the acidity of the wine would be far too high.   If you visit the Veronese vineyards of northern Italy which produce that superb white wine, *Soave Bolla*, just before the vintage and taste the grapes, you will find them, at about 20 per cent (or more) sugar, sickeningly sweet.

In short, your palate is a misleading instrument for judging ripeness.   So what do you do?

There is an instrument you can buy which enables you to draw a few drops of juice from ripening grapes and read off the sugar content.   But there is very little point in doing so because it is inconceivable that grapes would ever, in our climate, become too ripe for good wine.   Can a grape be too ripe to make good wine?   Yes, if you want dry wine.   No known wine yeast can survive in an environment which is more than about 16 per cent alcohol.   If, therefore, the grapes have a sugar content in excess of 32 per cent, sugar is left in the wine

161

and it will be sweet.   But this simply does not happen in our climate.

The solution to this problem is simple.   Leave your vintage to the last possible moment provided the grapes are not being attacked by moulds.   Your enemy is rain.   If the weather is fine but cold in late October, good: a touch of frost will enhance the quality of your wine.

Year three and for ever thereafter

Winter: prune as follows:

Cut out, as near the point of its origin as you can, the whole cane and its side shoots which have borne fruit.   You are now left with exactly what you had a year ago: two six foot canes tied to the bamboo.   Do what you did last year.   Bend the best of the pair down to the lower wire, tie it in place, and cut it off at the point where it meets the neighbouring vine.   Then cut the other down to 3 buds.

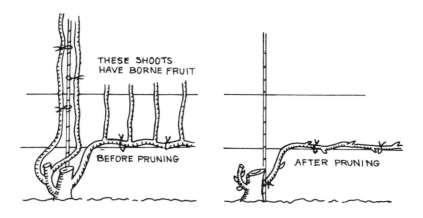

Remember: grape vines bear their fruit on the wood, and only on the wood, of one year's growth.   So, if you cut back to older wood—no grapes.

Quantity and quality

Since the two tall canes you grow each year to produce the following year's fruiting and replacement canes, spring from a spur of one-year-old wood, both may be, probably will be,

162

fruitful.   Remove the flower clusters on those canes: you want good wine, not a lot of fluid which will taste nasty and give you a stomach-ache.   The very finest wines are made in relatively cold climates: but only at the expense of quantity.

Every one of your vines could yield much more fruit than the method I have described will yield.   By allowing far more growth to remain when you prune, doubling the length of the bearing cane or allowing for two bearing canes etc, etc, you could get at least three times as many bunches of grapes.   But the more bunches you allow the vine to bear, the poorer will be the quality of your wine.   I repeat, without apology, the management of grape vines must be adapted to climate and soil.   The northern limit for viticulture is supposed to be latitude 50° N.: all Britain is above that limit.   We can produce good wine: but not if we go for quantity.

The wine-grower and the law

If you grow grapes and make wine for your own consumption, and that of your family and friends at home, the Excise man will not trouble you, though when he gets to hear about what you are up to, he may call to make sure that you understand the law and are not cheating the department.

If, however, you are going in for wine making on a considerable scale, as a number of growers have done since the 1950s, and propose to market your wine, then your house will have to become 'bonded' premises and excise duty paid on the alcohol content of the wine consigned from your house to the buyer.

I do not propose to give you directions here as to what you should do if you plan to 'go commercial'.   This book is about growing for subsistence in the first place not for sale.   If you are planting a vineyard, subsistence or commercial, you will, in any case, do well to become a member of the English Vineyards Association, York House, 199, Westminster Bridge Road, London SE1, who will give you the information you require.   You should also get in touch with the nearest Customs and Excise officer, who will be helpful.

Britain's membership of the EEC has, however, introduced certain problems new to Britain into the lives of the commercial wine-growers.   (The grower who is not selling any wine is not affected).   EEC rules affect the commercial grower at two points: there are certain hybrid vine varieties which he is not allowed to plant, though other hybrids are (and all the *cépages nobles*), permitted. Secondly, it is illegal under EEC rules, to add sugar to wine *after* fermentation. Sugar, in permitted quantities and of permitted quality, may be added to the *must* to raise its sugar content and therefore the ultimate alcohol content of the wine, but it may not be added after the wine has been made, nor is it legal to do any kind of chemical tampering with the wine.

Unfortunately, at the time of writing, British officials have not yet familiarised themselves with the EEC rules: thus, an official was sent to one successful commercial vineyard in 1973 to forbid the use of sugar in wine making though it was being used perfectly legally under EEC rules. The distinguished *vigneron* in question had some difficulty in convincing the bureaucrats that they had not done their homework.

At all events, the would-be commercial grower should take the trouble to discover both the British and European rules of wine growing and wine making.

Books on making wine

Wine Making and Brewing, F. W. Beech and A. Pollard, *The Amateur Winemaker*, South Street, Andover, Hants. 1970.

Basic Oenology A. Massel, Heidelberg Publishers Ltd, 11 Southampton Row, London WC 1.

Wines from your vines W. B. N. Poulter, *The Amateur Winemaker*, South Street, Andover, Hants.

For readers who want something rather more advanced and professional and who can read French, I commend
Traité de Vinification L. Benvegnin, E. Capt. and G. Piguet, The Librairie Payot, 10, Rue Centrale, 1003 Lausanne, Switzerland.
and, for German-readers:
Die Technologie des Weines G. Troost, Eugen Ulmer Verlag, Gerokstr. 19, Postfach 1032, Stuttgart, West Germany.

CHAPTER 11   GROWING YOUR OWN TOBACCO

The genus *Nicotiana* is an American one.   All 45 species were confined, with one (Australian) exception, to America, chiefly Central and Tropical America.   How many of these species were smoked by the native Americans is not clear but as far as I know only two have been of any importance commercially since the introduction of smoking to the Old World after about 1520, and the introduction of tobacco plants to several European countries.   They are *Nicotiana tabacum,* a tropical plant but one which, being an annual, can be grown in the temperate zone during the frost free months of the year; and *Nicotiana rustica,* a native of Mexico and Texas and probably the first species to be introduced into Europe.

The Spaniards were the first Europeans to cultivate tobacco, in Haiti.   Jean Nicot, French Consul in Lisbon, saw the plants being cultivated in Portugal in 1560 and, having introduced some into France, was honoured by the botanists who took his name for the genus then new to European science — hence *Nicotiana.* But in fact Brazilian tobacco was being grown in France as early as 1556.

Tobacco plants, probably *N. rustica,* were introduced into England late in the 16th century.   It was in use here medically (as snuff) before 1570.   Smoking came later and was at first a very expensive luxury, for tobacco at the end of the 16th century cost the equivalent of three or four pounds sterling per ounce.   But there is no climatic or technical reason why a tobacco growing industry should not have been established here as it was in France as well as in more southerly countries.   It grows very well here.   It is true that sun drying of tobacco is usually impossible in Britain; but much commercial

165

tobacco is, in any case, kiln dried and since the drying of hops in kilns is a technique which was used here before the introduction of tobacco, the commercial crop could have been kiln dried.

Two forces prevented the establishment of commercial tobacco growing in England. King James the First and Sixth detested smoking and considered it a filthy habit; and it was easier to grow and cure it in the summer climate of Virginia.   It was, moreover, economically expedient to leave the Virginian colonists a cash-crop which they could grow without competition from the mother country and so have the means to buy, in Britain, the commodities they required for the establishment of civilized life in the colony.

For some years I grew a crop of tobacco for my own use, in East Kent.   It was not much trouble; I gave it up chiefly because I wanted the land for my strawberry and melon trials which took up a lot of room; secondly because I disliked handling the curiously sticky, clammy plants.

Varieties.   A number of seedsmen now offer seeds of *Nicotiana tabacum* and *N. rustica* varieties suitable for growing in Britain—Dobies of Llangollen, Thompson and Morgan of Ipswich, Suttons of Reading and others.   But I am bound to say that the amateur tobacco grower's wisest plan is to obtain either seed or plants in due season from the Tilty Tobacco Centre and Tobacco Curing Co-operative, Dunmow, Essex (see below).   This body, originally the Amateur Tobacco Growers Association founded in 1948 by Mr Hugh Cuthbertson, can and will advise on which tobacco variety is most suitable for your local conditions and to suit your taste in tobacco, and will sell you the seeds or plants in question.

No reason, of course, why you should not try some of the seedsmen's offerings as well from the start, or when you have more experience of tobacco growing.

Tobacco growing and the law

Until 1948 it was illegal to grow tobacco in Britain.   But in that year the law was changed and allowed gardeners to grow tobacco on their own land for their own consumption and that of their family, provided that it was cured and processed on the premises and none of it was sold.

166

Now although you can, and thousands of growers do, cure their own tobacco, it is very difficult to get a good, palatable, smoke that way. In 1949 the Customs and Excise authorities made a further concession: it permitted a non-profitmaking association of tobacco growers, registered with and regulated by HM Customs and Excise, to receive from each of its members up to 25 lbs of leaf per annum, for 'curing'. The leaf has to be dried by the grower, but its fermentation process is carried out by the Association.

I have mentioned the only one of these Associations—the Tilty Tobacco Curing Co-operative of Dunmow, Essex, of which I have personal knowledge, above. Their secretary will let you know what it costs to join and how much you will pay for curing (about 3p an ounce). There is also an organisation in Scotland: The Scottish Amateur Tobacco Growing and Curing Association, 39 Milton Road, Kirkcaldy, Fife. As you will be paying no Excise duty, the saving will be substantial.

Members of the co-operative send in their leaf in November or December; and receive back their cured tobacco in spring or early summer. But they have to do their own shredding—the Co-operative sells a shredding machine.

Cultivation

Sow the seed during March in trays of John Innes No. 1 sterilised compost, under glass and maintain a temperature of 65 °F. The seed of tobacco is very minute and this makes it very difficult to sow it thinly enough to make the seedlings easy to handle at the next stage. To overcome this difficulty, fill a tea cup with fine, dry, silver sand and add a couple of pinches of seed: stir very thoroughly to distribute the seed through the sand. Spread the sand on the surface of the compost and water it *very lightly*, using a very fine rose. Shade the trays with a sheet of cardboard until the seeds germinate.

As soon as the seedlings are big enough to handle, prick them out into boxes of John Innes, No. 3 compost, at 2 inches apart.

Tobacco is a tender annual (or biennial grown as an annual) and will not stand frost. So the boxes of seedlings, kept free of weeds and moderately watered, should be kept in the greenhouse or under cloches until all danger of frost is over, usually mid May in the south and the end of May in the north.　But it is a good idea to move the boxes into the open on fine days, moving them back into safety at sunset, so as to begin and prolong the hardening-off process.　Towards the end of this period, unless there is any danger of frost, the boxes should be left out day and night.

If you don't want to do all this yourself and have joined the Tilty Co-operative, you can order you plants from them during the winter.　They will be delivered by post, for planting out, in May.

Tobacco makes a large plant: it will grow to four feet tall or more, having a stout, sappy main stem and a number of branches at or near the base, making it bushy.　So the plants need plenty of room.　Plant out in the second half of May or, in the north, in the first week of June—earlier if the weather and weather forecast permit—2 feet apart in rows 3 feet apart, planting firmly and watering in if the weather is dry.　It is useless to plant later than about 10 June: *Nicotianas* are long-day plants and their growth is slowed down as the days begin to shorten.　Irrigation may be necessary to prevent flagging during the first few days if the weather happens to be dry and warm.

Keep the tobacco rows free of weeds by hoeing between the plants and rotovating between the rows; or by rotovating in both directions.　Keep an eye on the plants for the appearance of flower buds: flowering and seed making take a lot of a plant's energy whereas what we want is as many large leaves as possible.　So as soon as flower buds appear, pinch out at once.　Another practice is to begin pinching out when the plants are 3 feet tall, forcing all the energy which would have been used to make the top 12 or 18 inches of growth, and the flowers, into increasing the weight of the leaf crop.　Under British conditions this is not usually sound practice.　It is certainly a mistake in wet, cool, or wet, warm summers, but can be effective in our rare hot, dry summers.　Bear in mind the following: your aim is to get the greatest possible weight of large, mature leaves but of a certain fine quality, not simply the hugest, thickest, coarsest leaves possible.　You do want to divert the energy which the plant would normally use to make flowers and seed, into leaf growth; but if you do so too soon, your tobacco will be coarse and rank; too late, then you will get a poor crop.　A safe compromise is to allow the plants to make

168

flower buds and wait till the most advanced bud is showing a sliver of colour. Then pinch out the whole inflorescence including two or three of the small leaves below it. Thereafter, keep on pinching out side shoots as fast as they develop. There is a refinement of this practice called 'priming': the small leaves low down on the plant are removed which has the effect of enlarging the large ones.

Harvesting

Harvesting is as late as possible: the season is, in England, rather too short for tobacco-growing simply because the plants cannot be planted out until late May. You can either cut down the whole plants and hang them to dry slowly in a dry shed; or you can harvest the leaves separately. (Turkish and other fine tobaccos depend for their quality on keeping the leaves picked from different parts of the plants in separate groups because their position on the plant determines their quality).

If you harvest leaf by leaf you begin in September, picking the lower leaves when their green begins to fade towards yellow. The harvested leaves now have to be dried and for this purpose you need a very dry, airy shed, barn, sun porch or greenhouse. Hang each leaf separately so that air can circulate all round it.

The process is continued until the end of October in most regions of Britain. The whole crop must be under cover before the first frost. The top leaves are harvested last. It is probably a sound plan to finish the job by mid October and it is good garden hygiene to dig up the roots and burn them with all rubbish leaves and bits of stalk you may have rejected.

When the leaves are dry you can 'hank' them—put them together in flat bundles with a wire through the tops of the stalks. They will then be ready for dispatch—on or after 1 November, not before, to the Co-operative for curing. Or if you are going to do your own curing (don't try it), then you can start now.

Curing

Tobacco *can* be smoked uncured but it tastes and smells disgusting. Curing was formerly a process of slow fermentation

G

in stacks over a long period of time. This process has been shortened by a technique of slow 'cooking' in kilns which was invented in Holland. It takes 4 or 5 months and accomplishes more or less the same chemical changes as the older process.

Those who wish to try curing at home can obtain instructions for doing so from the Tilty Co-operative.

Pests and diseases

Apart from White Fly at the greenhouse stage, easily disposed of with an aphicide spray, whose residues will be washed away in the course of the season's exposure to rain and irrigation water, tobacco is most unlikely to be attacked by any pests or diseases in Britain.

The most serious disease of tobacco is a virus disease known as 'Mosaic' because of the characteristic symptom, leaf mottling. While it is very rare in Britain, it is just possible that the virus is identical with the one which causes Cucumber Mosaic and quite certain that it can infect tomatoes and, probably, capsicums.

There is controversy whether virus can or cannot be carried from plant to plant on the gardener's hands. I rather doubt it, but there's no harm in taking the precaution of washing the hands in hot water with plenty of soap before and after handling these tobacco plants.

CHAPTER 12   GROWING NUTS

For a number of reasons nut growing is not included under any of the general headings: its demands on space, time, patience and skill make it unsuitable for the gardener whose principal interest is to get the maximum amount and diversity of food out of his garden for the minimum of effort.

But for the vegetarian who has not, indeed, an allotment but a garden of his own attached to a house he proposes to continue to live in, the case is different.   Nuts are important in his diet and there is no reason why he should not cultivate them.

Filberts and cobnuts

Both are cultivated varieties of *Corylus avellana*, the wild hazel-nut, developed thousands of years ago in Asia Minor.   Cobs are short, fat and round; filberts are longer and flatter.   Lambert's Filbert, otherwise and misleadingly known as Kentish Cob is the best variety to grow.

Nut trees can be grown as standards, which calls for grafting; as untrained bushes, which is easy; and as trained bushes which yield the largest and finest nuts in the greatest quantity, but is not easy.   I shall deal only with the two kinds of bushes.

Untrained bushes

The natural bush has a number of trunks from the ground, for these bushes sucker freely.   The main stems produce branches and the branches produce much ramified, fine, wiry twigs and it is on these that the nuts are borne.

The young bushes should be planted in November in soil

which has been well manured with compost (or farmyard manure), 12 feet apart in the row. Thereafter shaping is confined to removing surplus suckers—five or six main stems are quite enough; and cutting out branches which overcrowd the centre of the bush. No other pruning need be done on these untrained bushes, but if you want to improve the size and quality of the nuts follow the pruning routine for trained bushes.

It is a mistake to let grass and weeds grow round nut trees. Keep the soil between the trees and between the rows hoed or rotovated clean and dress it annually with compost.

Unfortunately nuts flower in late February or early March (in very mild winters, flowering may be in January); unfortunately because the weather may be very cold and spoil the flowers. Also unfortunately the male and female flowers don't always open at the same time: if they don't you will get no nuts.

Male and female flowers grow on the same bush: the male flowers are grouped in conspicuous golden-yellow catkins which, when mature, release clouds of pollen. Some of this falls on the female flowers: these are little tufts made conspicuous by the stigmas which are like scarlet plumes protruding from the tufts.

Although the best filberts are obtained from Kentish Cob (Lambert's Filbert) this variety does not produce many catkins so every fourth bush should be of the variety Cosford or Pearson's Prolific (if you can get them), which produce plenty of catkins. Probably the pollen from wild hazel nut catkins can fertilise the female flowers of cultivated nuts.

You will get some nuts after 3 or 4 years, but not a full crop, until the bushes are six years old.

The ground between the bushes and rows should be used for vegetable catch crops; nuts are not reliable croppers so a secondary use should be made of the land to avoid waste.

Trained bushes

Begin with suckers—single, rooted stems about 3 feet tall. Plant them 12 feet apart in the row in richly-manured soil in November. Cut them back at once to 18 inches tall. In the following spring and summer they will produce from four to eight branches which should grow vigorously. Aim to get six evenly distributed round the trunk. If any tree produces more than six, cut out the surplus ones.   In the case of those which produce fewer than six, you will have to cut back one or more of the branches which have grown, to two buds; as both will grow, you will have two branches where you had only one before.

The bushes should be pruned in February.   Shorten all six branches by half their length, or thereabouts, cutting to a bud.   What you are aiming to make is a permanent structure consisting of a stout, short trunk and six stout 'branches' 6 feet long radiating from it.

Every year, for the first four years at least, repeat this shortening of the six main branches in February.   Allow no more branches from the trunk to grow; and remove any suckers as soon as they appear.

The annual cutting back of the main branches means that it takes longer to get the finished tree completed, but also that the branches will be much stouter.   It has another effect also: it promotes the production on the branch of laterals, that is side shoots, which bear nuts.

Even when you have your bushes made, pruning in February has to be done.   By then the flowers—female tufts, and male catkins—will be visible; cut each side shoot back to the outermost flower or flower bud.

During the season, side shoot growth may be vigorous. Look over the bushes in August and shorten any particularly strong side shoots back to eight buds not by cutting but by breaking, leaving the broken-off end hanging by its bark.   Then, in the following February, shorten these back again to three buds.

When I was training nut trees I found that whereas I wanted a dished shape like this:

I was getting something more like this:

So to each bush I fixed six long bamboos stuck into the ground and bound at their crossing point, like this:

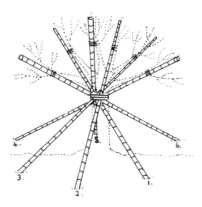

I then bent the branches downwards and tied them to the canes and maintained this structure in place until the branches had been trained to the required angle.

Walnuts

The common Walnut, *Juglans regia,* grown from seed will not bear any fruit until it is at least ten years old and probably not until it is 15 years old.   Moreover the size and quality of the nuts is a gamble. Therefore you should plant only grafted trees, the stock being a seedling, the scion taken from a tree of a variety known for performance and quality. Certain French varieties which can be had from the best English nurseries bear the largest and best nuts and begin to do so in their seventh year.

The trees thrive best on a deep, rich loam. Plant at least 50 feet apart, and stake firmly for the first three years. They respond to clean cultivation and annual mulching with compost during their first 5 or 6 years. After that they can be 'grassed down' but the grass must be kept mown short and the mowings left in place to rot down.

Although walnut trees are hardy in the general sense of the word, the young leaves and shoots are very apt to be seriously damaged by spring frosts. It is, therefore, quite useless, to plant them in 'frost pockets'—low-lying sites into which cold air drains from higher land on frosty nights in April and early May. They need a site which is as free from the spring frost danger as possible.

Little or no pruning should be needed but if any pruning has to be done in order to balance the head of a misshapen tree, it must be done either when the tree is quite dormant—December or January; or when it is in full leaf in mid summer. Pruned in spring, the cuts will bleed copiously and this bleeding weakens the tree.

Chestnuts

Sweet chestnuts, *Castanea sativa*, can be grown anywhere in Britain but crops of good nuts are unlikely excepting in the warmer parts of the country. The largest nuts are to be had from certain French varieties, if you can get them, *eg Marron de Lyon*, *Gros Merle*, and *Paragon*. Scions of these can be grafted onto ordinary seedlings of chestnut. Fully developed ripe nuts can only be expected in years of good summer and warm autumn.

Trees will grow in any soil excepting chalk or where the subsoil is a soluble limestone, do best in a deep, rich loam, are quite hardy, appreciate firm staking, clean cultivation and continual mulching with compost for the first four or five years, and should be planted 50 feet apart. They are very resistant to

175

drought but will grow faster if well watered when still young.

Sweet (or Spanish) chestnuts flower very late, in July. All the lower catkins bear only male flowers, but the higher ones bear several female flowers at the base and these give rise to nuts.

Pruning, in the ordinary sense, is not necessary. The only pruning ever likely to be needed would be to shape the head of the tree if it shows a tendency to grow lop-sided, which is not likely.

Almonds

Because the almond tree is grown in Britain as an ornamental tree, it is virtually impossible to buy trees of known performance as nut bearers. It is true that given a suitably warm, frost-free early spring, the almond trees commonly grown here will produce fruits which, given a good summer, will develop good nuts. Better results can be ensured by getting, from Italy or Spain, scions of a variety of tried performance for grafting or budding onto either an almond seedling or a plum seedling stock. But producing good almonds in Britain is a gamble, justified by the beauty of the tree in spring.

Almond trees intended to bear nuts need a high site to minimise the risk of frost damage to the flowers in March/April. Like most species of the genus *Prunus* they like lime in the soil. They are very tolerant of drought.

Plant at least 15 feet apart, stake firmly and keep up a routine of clean cultivation and annual mulching with compost during the trees' early years.

Keep pruning to a minimum and do any which is necessary in the spring or summer, not the autumn or winter. This will minimise the risk of infection by silver-leaf fungus.

Almond trees are as susceptible to the peach leaf curl disease as are the peaches to which they are so closely related. They must, therefore, be very thoroughly sprayed in February when flower buds are swelling, with either a copper lime or a lime sulphur fungicide. If heavy rain follows shortly after spraying, spray again.

How important is all this?

What can I say?   The old, experienced gardener gets good results by applying to the problem the kind of knowledge, known as judgement or intuition which is acquired by practice and cannot be put into words or taught deliberately.   Remember the witches in *Macbeth*?   'By the pricking of my thumbs, Something wicked this way comes.'   I am trying to give you the means to make up for the fact that you are not a peasant.   I know from my own experience that a born-and-bred cockney—and, by extension, any other townsman—can, by bringing a fresh mind unencumbered by bucolic lore, cut corners and get results when growing food, which the old hands thought impossible.   But the difference in crop per square yard between the gardener who without any justifying experience and, in his heart, despising the countryman, goes at the job in the any-bloody-fool-can-do-it spirit, and gardeners who, in default of experience, take experienced advice, can be measured like this:

Output of food per annum from 300 square yards of good garden soil by a trained horticultural scientist working single handed	10 tons per acre
Average output by a amateur gardener conscientiously applying tried and true methods	8 tons per acre
Average output of the slapdash gardener unwilling to apply his mind to a task he regards as a way of getting exercise	4 tons per acre

177

Guesswork? Maybe, but I'd lay all Lombard Street to a China orange that the figures are not far out.

My father, a very good gardener, rest his soul, taught me, 'If a thing's worth doing, it's worth doing well.' When I was nineteen I heard Bernard Shaw say that if a thing was worth doing, it was worth doing badly. Do your gardening your way; I promise not to say, 'I told you so'.

APPENDIX I CALCULATING IRRIGATION REQUIREMENTS

I'll begin by disposing of an illusion: that all Britain is a wet country and irrigation is not necessary.

There are parts of Britain west of the Pennines and in the south west where this is true. But the whole eastern side of Britain, with a mean annual rainfall of between 20 and 30 inches, much of it falling at the wrong time of year from the gardener's point of view, does not provide plants with sufficient water for optimum results, and the gardener should, therefore, if he has the means and is allowed to, make up this deficiency at certain times of year. I say, 'if he is allowed to' because, although sufficient water falls as rain, or snow, on Britain to supply far more than our maximum water requirement, it has been so badly mismanaged (not by water authorities but by Government neglect of their recommendations), that until the water-conservation projects now in hand are complete and the country has what amounts to a water grid, parts of Britain will from time to time suffer droughts, and consequently water-use restrictions, more appropriate to the Middle East than to an island with a reputation for being dismally wet.

How plants use water

Plants take in water through their roots and when atmospheric humidity is above a certain level, through their leaves. When atmospheric humidity falls below that level, the leaves transpire water; in other words, the plants sweat. That is fine for just as long as their intake through the roots exceeds or equals their output by transpiration. But if the rate of transpiration exceeds the rate of intake the whole metabolic process is slowed down, growth is checked, and the plants wilt. The grower suffers a loss. Soil water scientists use a term, the 'root constant' to define the maximum soil water deficit which can be built up without checking transpiration.

The grower's object must therefore be to maintain soil water at a level just above the 'root constant', so that transpiration, and hence growth, is never checked.

Traditionally this is done by judgement, a sort of guesswork inspired by experience and intuition. And most growers will continue to use that means so that some will get it about right, some will keep their plants short of what they need, and others will waste water by giving too much. I am writing this Appendix for the benefit of those who would like to know if there is a more 'scientific' way of dealing with the problem and who may even consider using it.

'Field capacity' and the 'pumping' power of plants

Above the water table there is water in two places in ordinary garden soil: mingled with air in the spaces between the soil particles; and as a skin of water enclosing each soil particle. During and after heavy rain the soil will be temporarily water-logged, that is to say that the air in the spaces between the soil particles is driven out by water. If this condition persisted, the plants would drown, for their roots must have air. Hence the importance of drainage; the surplus water drains away into the deeper levels, maintaining the level of the water table which is itself draining into ditches and thence into rivers, canals, lakes and the sea. As the soil dries, air is drawn in again and the roots can breathe. If this drainage were complete the soil would become bone dry and the plants would die of thirst. Hence the importance of having a water-retentive soil.

Now let us suppose drought conditions; plants can easily draw up the water which is between the soil particles; and some of the water which forms a skin round the soil particles. But not all of it. An apparently dessicated soil in which all the plants have withered for want of water is found on analysis still to contain a substantial quantity of water. The plants have been unable to use it because they cannot overcome the surface tension holding it in the soil particles.

180

From this it will be obvious that a soil is at optimum condition for plant health and growth when, following drainage, it is holding all the water which its nature allows it to hold against the force of gravity.   A soil in this condition is said to be at 'field moisture capacity' or 'field capacity' for short.   The grower's problem then is to maintain his garden at field capacity.   Rainfall helps him to do so, but what are the forces working against him?

In the first place, transpiration of water by his plants, already referred to; this is more or less measurable and the rate of transpiration depends upon the weather and the time of year.   Broadly speaking and on average there is a soil moisture deficit due to transpiration in May, June, July and August.   This deficit is defined as 'the amount of water necessary to restore the soil to field capacity'.

In order to calculate that amount we need to know two figures: (1) monthly loss of water due to transpiration, and (2) monthly measured rainfall.   Subtract (2) from (1) and you have the net loss of water, that is the soil moisture deficit.   Rainfall is easily measured by means of a simple rain gauge.   As to the transpiration loss, it is sufficiently accurate to make use of long term averages for potential transpiration, established by the Meteorological Office—see the table below.

Area	Apr.	May	June	July	Aug.	Sept.	Summer Total
			in.				*in.*
West Lancashire ...	2·10	3·10	3·65	3·75	3·20	1·90	17·70
Cheshire and South-west Lancashire	2·10	3·00	3·50	3·50	3·05	1·75	16·90
Fens	2·05	3·10	3·75	3·60	3·05	1·65	17·20
South Cambridgeshire	2·05	3·25	3·85	3·75	3·10	1·70	17·70
Bedfordshire	2·05	3·20	3·80	3·80	3·10	1·70	17·65
Herefordshire	2·10	3·10	3·70	3·75	3·10	1·70	17·45
Worcestershire ...	2·00	3·00	3·60	3·60	3·10	1·60	16·90
South Cornwall ...	2·10	3·10	3·50	3·35	3·15	1·80	17·00
Somerset	1·95	3·00	3·45	3·65	3·25	1·65	16·95
South Hampshire and West Sussex	1·90	3·40	3·85	4·05	3·20	1·65	18·05
Kent	2·00	3·25	4·00	4·05	3·30	1·80	18·40

Specimen Monthly Averages of Potential Transpiration in the Main Horticultural Areas

Here is a simple example: we may take it that the garden soil will be at field capacity on April 30. The potential transpiration loss from a garden full of crops during May is 3 inches, expressed as rainfall equivalent. On 31 May your rain gauge shows that during May rainfall was 1.5 inches. The deficit is, therefore, 1.5 inches and that, on 31 May, is the rainfall equivalent you need to apply in order to restore your garden to field moisture capacity.

Thus what you now need to know is the amount of water measured in gallons which is equal to 1.5 inches of rainfall on an area of 300 square yards.

What does '1 inch rainfall' mean?

An inch of rainfall means as much rain as, if none of it drained away after falling, would leave a sheet of water one inch deep all over the area where it had fallen.

Come back for a moment to our 300 square yards garden. Since rainfall equal to one inch of rain would leave a sheet of water one inch deep all over if none drained away, then an inch of rainfall can be calculated in terms of gallons, thus:

One gallon = 277 cubic inches
One square yard = 1296 square inches therefore
300 square yards = 1296 x 300 = 388,800 square inches
388,800 square inches x 1″ deep = 388,800 cubic inches
388,800 ÷ 277 = <1400 gallons

So, in order to apply 1 inch of rain-equivalent to your 300 square yards of garden, by irrigation, note the figure recorded on your water meter, turn on the irrigation system, shifting the sprinkler hose at regular intervals, and leave it on until your water-meter shows a figure 1400 gallons higher than when you began.

The gardener is bound to have a water-meter in any case since the water supply authority meters all water for irrigation use, with a meter on the premises for the purpose of invoicing the consumer. But he will also need a rain gauge, which is not an expensive item, and he will require the table on p. 181, which gives him specimen Monthly Averages of Potential Transpiration in the main horticultural areas. Using these two instruments and the table he will produce a water Balance sheet, month by month from April to September: you will find an example on p. 187: it is based on our unit plot of 300 square yards.

This method, based on the averages table, while it is very much more exact than mere guessing or gardener's judgement, is rough-and-ready when compared with the Estimated Method. Gardeners who wish to use this very much more sophisticated method should procure and consult the Stationery Office pamphlet *Potential Transpiration* published for the Ministry of Agriculture, Fisheries and Food.

The concept 'potential transpiration' and 'frequency of irrigation need'

Potential transpiration is the transpiration which, based on fairly long-term averages, is to be expected in any given period. Map 1, below, shows Potential April-September transpiration in inches of rainfall equivalent for all England and Wales.

You will wish to know the extent to which this loss of soil water is made good by summer rainfall in your part of England and Wales. Map 2 shows you this.

Map 3, derived from Maps 1 and 2, indicates the probable frequency of irrigation need all over England and Wales. From Map 3 you can check my assertion that, popular opinion of our climate notwithstanding, irrigation is necessary to maintain field moisture capacity—the optimum condition for plant growth—even in the wet west in more than 5 years out of ten, and in only just under 9 years out of 10 in the east, south-east and Thames Valley.

Maps 1, 2, and 3, and the table on p. 181 are from *The Calculation of Irrigation Need*, the Ministry of Agriculture's Technical Bulletin No. 4, 1954, by permission of the Controller HMSO.

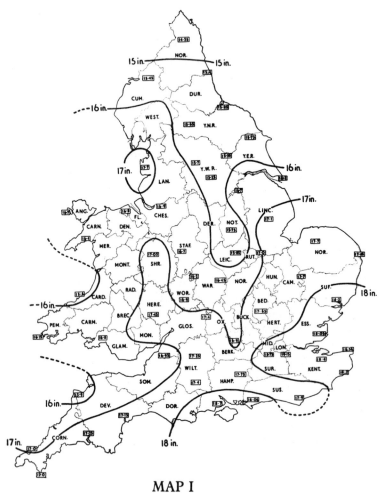

MAP I
Average Summer Potential Transpiration
(April-September) for period 1930-1949 (in inches)

6"

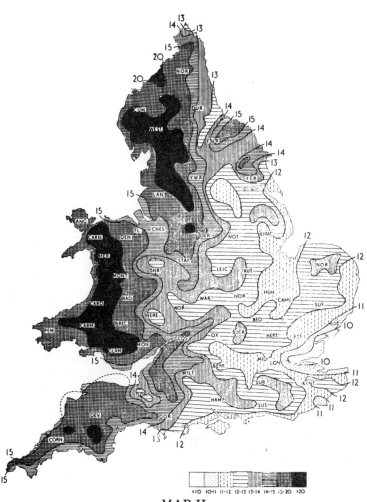

MAP II
Average Summer Rainfall
(April-September) for period 1881-1915 (in inches)

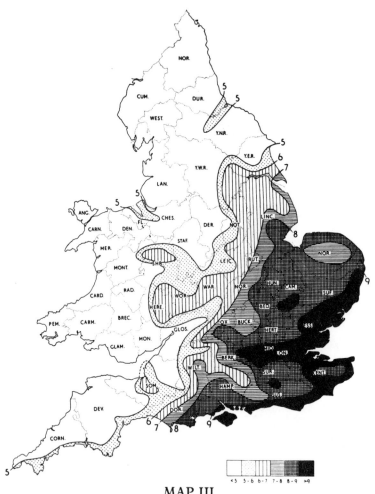

MAP III
Frequency of Irrigation Need
(Years in Ten)

Month	Potential transpiration less tolerable deficit	Rainfall during month	Irrigation used during month	Irrigation need at end of month	
				Inches	Gallons
April	1.55 inches	1.80 inches	NIL	NIL	NIL
	An excess of 0.25 inches have fallen during the month: thus no end-of-month irrigation is needed; the surplus will be carried off by drainage.				
May	2.65 inches	2.88 inches	NIL	NIL	NIL
	Once again, rainfall more than makes up for transpiration.				
June	3.05 inches	1.06 inches	0.49 inches	1.50	2100
	The sum is like this: 3.05 − 1.06 − 0.49 = 1.50 inches, the deficit at 31 May. So you must make this good by putting on 2,100 gallons of irrigation water.				
July	3.10 inches	1.90 inches	NIL	1.20	1680
August	2.55 inches	3.63 inches	NIL	NIL	NIL
September	1.55 inches	0.80 inches	0.80 inches	NIL	NIL

APPENDIX II   DEEP FREEZING VEGETABLES

Surpluses over and above what you need for immediate consumption have to be stored; and the modern way to store
vegetables is to put them into your deep freezer if you have
one.   When it comes to root vegetables, there is no point in
deep freezing them, for they are best kept in clamps, boxes of
sand in a dark, dry shed or, for that matter, in the case of
onions, hanging in trusses in some cool, frost-free, dry place
(see p. 66).   There is no point, either, in trying to keep brassica
crops in the deep freezer because you can be harvesting them
fresh from the garden throughout the winter.   Certain vegetables, celery for instance, cannot be kept in the deep freezer
because of their very high water-content.   We are, therefore,
left with peas and beans; and soft fruits.   I doubt very much
whether it is worth displacing meat, poultry and game from the
deep freezer to make room for peas and beans.   Why not,
instead, eat the vegetables which are in season in the winter?   Still, if you want to deep freeze peas and beans, you can
do so provided you grow suitable varieties.   I cannot give lists
of these because they would depend on which seedsman you
deal with.   However, the major seedsmen—people like Suttons, Carters, Dobbies, Thompson and Morgan, and others,
indicate in their catalogues those varieties which are suitable for
deep freeze storage.

   As to fruit, the only one which, in my opinion, is worth deep
freeze space, is the raspberry.

APPENDIX III   GLASS AND PLASTIC FOR PROTECTION

In order to raise seedlings of many vegetable garden crops such as lettuce, cabbages and the cabbage family, celery etc, earlier than you can do so on unprotected nursery beds in the open, and in order to raise your own stocks of tomato and other tender crops, you will need some kind of glass or plastic protection under which temperatures are higher in the daytime and frost excluded at night, during the late winter and early spring. Such protection has the added advantage of protecting seed beds and seedlings against excessively heavy rainfall and, incidentally, birds.   There are several categories to consider: heated greenhouses; cool greenhouses; cold frames; cloches; handlights; plastic tunnels.

Neither of the first two are justifiable investments on the 300 square yard plot unless you particularly want to grow greenhouse crops, of course.   But here I am considering glass simply as an ancillary 'tool' for the small vegetable grower.

Cold frames

A variety of kinds, shapes and sizes can be seen at any good garden centre.   I suggest one with a metal chassis and glass sides as well as top.   Place it so as to receive full sun, but provide yourself with the means of shading it during the heat of the day.   Ventilation by partial opening of the top-lights will be necessary on most spring days but the frame will usually have to be closed at night.   A frame measuring about 4 feet x 3 feet should be sufficient for your purpose.   During the summer when you will not need it for seedlings, it will hold a couple of cucumber plants.

189

Cloches

I have already covered these in Chapter 3 and there said why I prefer glass to plastic but if you buy plastic choose one of the stout, cellular kinds, not the thin sheet sort. Four 2 feet cloches will cover enough ground for your purpose. When not in use for raising seedlings early in the year, they can be used to cover cucumbers and, during the winter before seed-sowing starts, lettuces.

Handlights

There are on the market in good garden centres and hardware shops rigid plastic seed-trays covered with fitting rigid plastic domes. These are admirable for raising seedlings and with nine or ten of these you may well be able to manage without frames or cloches. They measure 14 x 9 inches or thereabouts. They can be placed on the ground, but it is more convenient to have them at waist height, on a simple one-plank bench.

Electrically-heated propagators

There are a number of electrically-heated propagation cases on the market and they are admirable for striking cuttings and raising seedlings. In my view, however, they are of more use to the shrub and flower gardener than to the vegetable gardener. For the man with a ten-rod plot who is growing only vegetables they are not a justifiable investment.

Warning on watering seedbeds, and seed trays under glass. More seed failures are caused by watering with a coarse 'rose' on the watering-can than by any other cause; small seeds are washed too deep into the soil to germinate; and tiny seedlings drowned. Use only the very finest 'rose' on the can or, better still, a syringe which produces a mist of water.

Glass on the larger plot

If you are cultivating a quarter acre plot then investment in a small greenhouse and two full ten-yard rows of cloches is justifiable. All the very early nursery work can then be done in seed-trays on the greenhouse bench; so can pricking-out and raising such crops as tomatoes to the point when they should be hardened off and planted out.   There should also be room for some tomatoes and peppers and perhaps a couple of cucumber plants though for them the conditions will not be ideal if they are right for tomatoes.   The most useful kind of greenhouse for your purpose will be glass to the ground and metal-framed.   As for the cloches they will be used on early and late lettuce, on early dwarf peas, and, in the summer, on melons.   If you grow autumn strawberries, then the cloches can go onto them in October.   Like other expensive plant, investment in cloches can only be justified if they are in constant use.

Plastic tunnels

These are now much used as cheap substitutes for cloches and greenhouses.   Apart from their cheapness and lightness, they seem to have one advantage over glass for certain crops, their high humidity retention.   They consist of a length or lengths of transparent plastic which is stretched and secured over a row of semicircular metal hoops which are stuck into the ground.   They have, of course, to be very firmly staked and guyed, like tents, otherwise they take off when the wind rises.   The small ones are about a foot or 15 inches high and are for raising early lettuces and other crops, or they can be used for cucumbers and melons.   The big ones are about 6 feet or more tall and cover a considerable area; thus tall crops like tomatoes can be grown in them as well as groundling crops.   The plastic has a short life: one or two seasons only.

APPENDIX IV   MACHINES AND SPRAYERS

Machine tools

Having tried most of the cultivating machines suitable for the
amateur with a garden or allotment big enough to justify
investment in an expensive piece of machinery, the one which I
recommend is the Wolseley-Webb Merrytiller.   There is a
range of models the lightest of which is called the Tri-
dent.   But to my mind the next up in the range, the Major is
better value for money.   It has a 3HP four-stroke engine which
does not give starting trouble.   You can use it for digging to 12
inches deep, or for shallow hoeing, the width of cultivating
being variable from 15 up to 37 inches by the quick and easy
addition of extra tines.   As well as the tine rotors, the machine
can be fitted with a range of other tools including a plough-
share, bull-dozer blade, and pronged weeder.   As prices are
rising as usual while I write this, it is difficult to give an exact
figure; but, with luck, you should not have to spend more than
£150.

Crop spraying

There are a number of devices on the market for pest-control
spraying from simple syringes to metal or plastic cylinders
holding a gallon or two gallons of spray liquid and which, once
pumped up, deliver a continuous spray through an adjustable
nozzle at the end of a lance.   In my experience both the pumps
and the nozzles give trouble sooner or later; but thorough
washing out and cleaning after use, and careful attention to
washing out the nozzles will reduce the incidence of break-
downs.   Spraying by muscle-power is always hard work which-

ever way you do it and you may consider an electric machine worthwhile. Black and Decker have on the market an easily portable electric compressor delivering air pressure to a light and handy sprayer. The equipment is, in fact, a modified paint-sprayer, and can also be used as such. For crop spraying it is admirable, delivering a very fine, dense mist of spray which is very effective indeed.

INDEX

Allotments, 3, 7-8
  double plot, 89-90, 103, 135-43
  economics of, 4-6, 84-5, 143
  importance of work, 177-8
  quarter of an acre plot, 144-50
  single plot, 62-86
Allotment Act (1922), 4, 7-8
Almonds, 176
Annual cycle,
  double plot, 135-43
  quarter of an acre plot, 149
  single plot, 62-84
Apples, 135, 147
  buying apple trees, 104
  growth, 106-9
  pests & diseases, 109-11
  planting, 105
  preparation for, 103-4
  spraying, 139
  tar-oil winter wash, 110
Apricots, 111
Artichokes, globe, 90
Artichokes, Jerusalem, 90-1
Aubergine (Egg plant), 99, 150

Basil, 55-6
Bay, 56
Beans, Broad, 38-9, 80, 81
Beans, Dwarf French, 39
Beans, Scarlet Runner, 39-40, 82
Beetroot, 41
Birds, 134, 141-2, 149
Blackberries, 111-12
Blackcurrants, 114-15, 135, 139, 140
Broccoli *see* Cauliflower
Brussels Sprouts, 41-2

Cabbage, 33, 42-3, 66
Cabbage, Chinese (Petsai), 94
Capsicum (Green Pepper), 99-100, 150
Cardoon, 93
Carrots, 33, 43-4, 66, 139
Catchcrops, 33, 139, 140, 141
Cauliflower, 44
Celery, 33, 44-5, 82
Chalk, 20
Chard, 94
Cherries, 112-14, 135, 139, 140
Chervil, 56-7
Chestnuts, 175-6
Chicory, *see* Witloof

Chives, 57
Chlorosis, 10
Cloches, 35, 190, 191
Cobnuts *see* Filberts
Cold Frames, 189
Compost, 15, 23, 27-8, 34, 81, 138, 147
Compost bins, 149
  construction of, 15-16
  use of, 16-18, 89, 141
Coriander, 57-8
Cress *see* Mustard & Cress
Crop spraying, 192-3
Cucumbers, 35, 100-1, 135, 139, 150

Damsons, 127
Deep Freezing, 188
Dibber, 33
Digging, 25-7, 81
Dill, 58
Diseases, 89-90
Drainage, 13, 180
Drill, 130

Egg Plant *see* Aubergine
Endive, 94-5

Fennel, 58, 95
Fertilizers, Chemical, 14-15, 21-3, 28-9
Fertilizers, Organic, 20-1
Figs, 115-16
Filberts & Cobnuts,
  trained bushes, 172-4
  untrained bushes, 171-2

Garlic, 59
Glass/Plastic protection, 189-91
Gooseberries, 116-17, 135, 139, 140
Grapes, dessert, 117-21
Grapes, wine, *see* Vineyards
Greenhouses, 150, 190-1
Green Peppers *see* Capsicum

Handlights, 190
Herbs, 55-61
Hoeing, 30-1, 80-3
Hyssop, 59

Irrigation *see* Watering

Kohl Rabi, 95

Layout, 62-6, 135-7, 146-50
Leeks, 45-6
Lettuce, 33, 46-7, 139, 147, 150
Lime, 19-20
Loam, 11, 13-15
Loganberries, 111-12

Manure, 14-15, 27-9
Marjoram, 59
Marrows, 47, 139
Melons, 35, 121-3, 139, 140, 141
Mint, 59
Mulch, 34
Mushrooms, 96
Mustard & Cress, 95-6

Nectarines, *see* Peaches
Nitrogen, 9, 21
Nursery bed, 31-2, 65
Nut growing, 171 *see also* individual
    species

Onions, 48-9, 66
Origanum *see* Marjoram

Parsley, 59-60
Parsnips, 49
Peaches, 123-6, 135, 138, 139, 141, 147
Pears, 126, 135, 139, 141, 147
Peas, 33, 34, 49-50, 81, 147, 188
Peas, Asparagus, 96
Peas, Mangetout, 95
Peat, 20
Pests, 89-90, 134, 141-2, 147, 192-3
Phosphorus, 22
Phylloxera, Vastatrix, 152-3, 156, 159
Pinching out, 32-3, 140, 141
Planting, 81, 82
Plastic tunnels, 191
Plums, 126-7, 135, 139-40, 141, 147
Potassium, 21
Potatoes, 50-2, 65, 66
Propagators, Electrically heated, 190
Pruning, 138, 140
    apples, 105-9, 138
    apricots, 111
    cherries, 113, 139
    figs, 116
    gooseberries, 117, 138
    grapes, 119-21, 138, 159-62
    peaches, 124, 139
    pears *see* apples
    plums *see* cherries
    raspberries, 128, 138
Pumpkins *see* Marrows

Quince, 127

Radishes, 33, 52, 139
Raspberries, 127-9, 138, 140, 188
Redcurrants, 115, 135
Rhubarb, 129, 138
Rosemary, 60
Rotation, 33-4
Rotovating, 138, 139, 140, 141, 147, 192
Rue, 60

Sage, 60
Salsify, 97
Savory, 60-1
Scorzonera, 97
Seeds
    hardening off, 32
    nursery bed, 31-2
    planting out, 32
    pricking out, 30-1
    seed bed, 30
    sowing, 29-30
Shallots, 52-3, 80
Soil
    analysis of, 23
    composition of, 9-10
    soil water, 12, 108
    sub-soil, 9, 11
    texture, 11, 14
    top-soil, 9, 11, 23
Spinach, 33, 53, 139, 140
Spinach Beet, 53
Sprayers, 192-3
Storage (of vegetables), 66, 188
Strawberries, 129-30, 132-3, 138-9, 140
    alpine s. (fraises des bois), 132
    autumn s. (perpetual), 131-2, 135, 141
    summer s., 130-1, 135
Swede, 53
Sweet corn, 53-4

Tea, 61
Thyme, 61
Time, 80-4, 142-3
Tobacco growing, 3, 146, 147, 150
    cultivation, 167-9
    curing, 167, 169-70
    harvesting, 169
    history of, 165-7
    tobacco & the law, 166-7
    varieties, 166
Tomatoes, 97-9, 101-2, 135, 139, 140,
    141, 150

Tools, 24-5
  dibbers, 33
  hoes, 30-1
  machine t., 192
Turnips, 33, 54-5, 139

Vineyards, 3, 117-18, 135, 138, 140,
  141, 146, 147, 151-2, 155-6
  American stock, 152-3
  bibliography, 164
  chaptalisation, 161-2
  disease control, 158-9
  greenhouse vines, 121
  history of, 151-2
  & the law, 163-4
  Old World stock, 152-3
  Phylloxera vastatrix, 152-3, 156
  Pinot Meuniere (Miller's Burgundy),
  156-7

Pinot noir, 156-7
  planting, 157-8
  preparation of land, 154-5
  pruning & cropping, 159-62
  quantity & quality, 162-3
  Riesling-Sylvaner, 156, 157
  Seyve-Villard, 156
  stockists, 157
  wall vines, 118-21
  yield, 153-4

Walnuts, 174-5
Wasps, 142
Watering, 35, 37, 140, 141, 147, 179
  amount needed, 182-3
  field capacity, 180-2
  use of water, 179-80
Whitecurrants *see* Redcurrants
Wineberries, 111-112
Witloof, 102